THE WAY AND ITS POWER

Lao Tzu's

TAO TÊ CHING

and

Its Place in Chinese Thought

Translated and Edited

by

ARTHUR WALEY

GROVE PRESS

New York

Translations by Arthur Waley
Published by Grove Press:
The Book of Songs
Monkey

This book has been accepted in the Chinese Translations Series of the United Nations Educational, Scientific, and Cultural Organization (UNESCO).

Printed in the United States of America

Library of Congress Catalog Card Number: 58-5092
ISBN 0-8021-5085-3

Grove Press
841 Broadway
New York, NY 10003

02   35 34 33 32 31 30 29

To
Leonard & Dorothy
Elmhirst

UNESCO COLLECTION OF REPRESENTATIVE
WORKS – CHINESE SERIES
This book has been accepted in the Chinese Translations
Series of the United Nations Educational, Scientific and
Cultural Organization (UNESCO)

CONTENTS

PREFACE

I HAVE noticed that general works[1] about the history of Man either ignore China altogether or relegate this huge section of mankind to a couple of paragraphs. One of my aims in this book is to supply the general anthropologist with at any rate an impetus towards including China in his survey. This does not however mean that the book is addressed to a small class of specialists; for all intelligent people, that is to say, all people who want to understand what is going on in the world around them, are 'general anthropologists', in the sense that they are bent on finding out how mankind came to be what it is to-day. Such an interest is in no sense an academic one. For hundreds of millennia Man was what we call 'primitive'; he has attempted to be civilized only (as regards Europe) in the last few centuries. During an overwhelmingly great proportion of his history he has sacrificed, been engrossed in omens, attempted to control the wind and rain by magic. We who do none of these things can hardly be said to represent normal man, but rather a very specialized and perhaps very unstable branch-development. In each of us, under the thinnest possible veneer of *homo industrialis*, lie endless strata of barbarity. Any attempt to deal with ourselves or others on the supposition that what shows on the surface represents more than the mere topmast of modern man, is doomed to failure.

And Man must be studied as a whole. Despite the lead

[1] e.g. A. M. Hocart's *The Progress of Man*, E. O. James's *Origins of Sacrifice*, both quite recent works.

given by unofficial historians there is still an idea that the Chinese are or at any rate were in the past so cut off from the common lot of mankind that they may be regarded almost as though they belonged to another planet, that sinology is in fact something not much less remote than astronomy and cannot, whatever independent interest or value it may have, possibly throw light on the problems of our own past. Nothing could be more false. It becomes apparent, as Chinese studies progress, that in numerous instances ancient China shows in a complete and intelligible form what in the West is known to us only through examples that are scattered, fragmentary and obscure.

It may however be objected that the particular book which I have chosen to translate is already well known to European readers. This is only true in a very qualified sense; and in order to make clear what I mean I must make a distinction which has, I think, too often been completely ignored. Supposing a man came down from Mars and seeing the symbol of the Cross asked what it signified, if he chanced to meet first of all with an archæologist he might be told that this symbol had been found in neolithic tombs, was originally a procreative charm, an astrological sign or I know not what; and all this might quite well be perfectly true. But it still would not tell the Man from Mars what he wanted to know—namely, what is the significance of the Cross to-day to those who use it as a symbol.

Now scriptures are collections of symbols. Their peculiar characteristic is a kind of magical elasticity. To successive generations of believers they mean things that would be paraphrased in utterly different words. Yet for

Preface

century upon century they continue to satisfy the wants of mankind; they are 'a garment that need never be renewed'. The distinction I wish to make is between translations which set out to discover what such books meant to start with, and those which aim only at telling the reader what such a text means to those who use it to-day. For want of better terms I call the first sort of translation 'historical', the second 'scriptural'. The most perfect example of a scriptural translation is the late Richard Wilhelm's version of the *Book of Changes*. Many critics condemned it, most unfairly in my opinion, because it fails to do what in fact the author never had any intention of doing. It fails of course to tell us what the book *meant* in the 10th century B.C. On the other hand, it tells us far more lucidly and accurately than any of its predecessors what the *Book of Changes* means to the average Far Eastern reader to-day.

There are several good 'scriptural' translations of the *Tao Tê Ching*. Here again I think Wilhelm's is the best, and next to it that of Carus.[1] But there exists no 'historical' translation; that is to say, no attempt to discover what the book meant when it was first written. That is what I have here tried to supply, fully conscious of the fact that to know what a scripture meant to begin with is perhaps less important than to know what it means to-day. I have decided indeed to make this attempt only because in this case the 'Man from Mars'—the Western reader—has been fortunate enough not to address his initial questions to the archæologist. More representative informants have long ago set before him the current (that is to say, the

[1] Or rather, of his Japanese collaborator.

13

medieval) interpretation of the *Tao Tê Ching*. I feel that
he may now be inclined to press his enquiries a little further; just as a tourist, having discovered what the swas-
tika means in Germany to-day, might conceivably become
curious about its previous history as a symbol. Funda-
mentally, however, my object is the same as that of
previous translators. For I cannot believe that the study
of the past has any object save to throw light upon the
present.

I wish also to make another, quite different, kind of
distinction. It has reference to two sorts of translation.
It seems to me that when the main importance of a work
is its beauty, the translator must be prepared to sacrifice
a great deal in the way of detailed accuracy in order to
preserve in the translation the quality which gives the
original its importance. Such a translation I call 'literary',
as opposed to 'philological'. I want to make it clear that
this translation of the *Tao Tê Ching* is not 'literary'; for the
simple reason that the importance of the original lies not
in its literary quality but in the things it says, and it has
been my one aim to reproduce what the original says with
detailed accuracy.

I must apologize for the fact that the introduction is
longer than the translation itself. I can only say that I
see no way of making the text fully intelligible without
showing how the ideas which it embodies came into
existence. The introduction together with the translation
and notes are intended for those who have no professional
interest in Chinese studies. The appendices to the introduction and the additional and textual notes are intended
chiefly for specialists. Thus the book represents a com-

Preface

promise—of a kind that is becoming inevitable, as facilities for purely specialist publication become more and more restricted.

After I had made my translation of the *Tao Tê Ching* and sketched out the introduction, I received Vol. IV of *Ku Shih Pien* and was delighted to find that a great contemporary scholar, Ku Chieh-kang, holds exactly the same views about the date and authorship of the work as I myself had formed.

The European scholars who have in recent years contributed most to our knowledge of ancient Chinese thought are Marcel Granet, Henri Maspero, J. J. L. Duyvendak, and Gustav Haloun. I have rather frequently expressed disagreement with M. Maspero; but this does not mean that I fail to recognize the high value of his work as a whole. Like all sinologues I owe a great debt to Bernhard Karlgren. The study of meanings is, in China at any rate, intimately associated with the study of sounds. Twenty years ago Chinese studies had reached a point at which, but for the laborious phonological researches undertaken by Karlgren, further progress, in almost every direction, was barred.

I owe a very special debt of gratitude to my friend, Dr. Lionel Giles, who read the proofs and made many suggestions and corrections. Finally, I should like to call attention to a peculiarity in my references to the *Book of Odes*. Instead of using the cumbrous and inconvenient system adopted by Legge, I number the poems 1–305, and hope that other scholars may be induced to follow suit.

INTRODUCTION

I WILL begin with a comparison. This is a passage from the *Book of History*: 'In the second year after the conquest of the Shang,[1] the king of Chou fell ill. . . . The two dukes said "let us reverently consult the tortoise on the king's behalf". But the king's other brother, the duke of Chou, said: "That is not the way to move the hearts of our ancestors, the former kings", and so saying the duke of Chou pledged his own life to ransom the king. He built three mounds on the same clearing; and for himself he made a mound to the south of these, and stood upon it, looking north. He set before him a disc of jade and in his hand he held a tablet of jade. Then he called upon the three dead kings, T'ai, Chi and Wên, and the scribe wrote his prayer upon a tablet. The duke said: "Your descendant Such-a-one[2] has met with a sharp and violent sickness. If this means that you three dead kings need some one to cherish and foster you in heaven, then take me instead of Such-a-one. For I am ready and well able to be very serviceable to ghosts and spirits; whereas your descendant the king is versed in few such arts, and would not be at all serviceable to ghosts and spirits. You, O kings, were charged by the Court of Ancestors to succour the four quarters of the land from end to end and to

[1] The Chou probably conquered the Shang early in the 10th century B.C. But the story which follows is a ritual theme (the brother who offers himself in place of the king-victim) and does not in reality belong to a particular period or instance. See, Frazer, *Golden Bough*, Pt. III, p. 160 seq. Also *Secret History of the Mongols*, Ch. XIV, 14.

[2] The king's personal name was taboo.

17

establish as best you might your sons and grandsons here on earth below. The people of the four quarters all worship and fear you. Do not frustrate the treasured mission that Heaven put upon you, and you too, O former kings, shall for ever find shelter and support.[1] I shall now ask the Great Tortoises[2] to tell me your decision. If you accept me instead of the king, I will dedicate[3] to you this disc of jade and this tablet of jade, and go home to await your command. But if you do not accept me, I shall hide away the tablet and the disc." He then consulted the three tortoises[4] and each was doubly favourable. He opened the locked-place and inspected the book of omens. This too was favourable. Then the duke of Chou said: "All is well! The king will come to no harm. I have secured a fresh mandate from the three former kings; we may make plans for an age-long futurity. Only wait; and you will see that to me they have certainly given heed." The duke of Chou went home and deposited the record of his prayer in a casket with metal clamps. By next day the king had recovered.'

The passage that I want to set in contrast to this is from *Mencius*: 'The Bull Mountain was once covered with lovely trees. But it is near the capital of a great state. People came with their axes and choppers; they cut the woods down, and the mountain has lost its beauty. Yet

---

[1] From the sacrifices and offerings of your descendants.

[2] Oracles were obtained from the tortoise by producing cracks in the shell by means of a red-hot stick or rod. These cracks were then interpreted as omens. Tortoise-divination is also practised in Africa. See H. A. Junod: *The Life of a S. African Tribe*, 2nd edit. 1927, II, 549.

[3] Here I follow Ku Chieh-kang, see *Ku Shih Pien* II, 69.

[4] One for each ancestor.

even so, the day air and the night air came to it, rain and dew moistened it. Here and there fresh sprouts began to grow. But soon cattle and sheep came along and broused on them, and in the end the mountain became gaunt and bare, as it is now. And seeing it thus gaunt and bare people imagine that it was woodless from the start. Now just as the natural state of the mountain was quite different from what now appears, so too in every man (little though they may be apparent) there assuredly were once feelings of decency and kindness; and if these good feelings are no longer there, it is that they have been tampered with, hewn down with axe and bill. As each day dawns they are assailed anew. What chance then has our nature, any more than that mountain, of keeping its beauty? To us too, as to the mountain, comes the air of day, the air of night. Just at dawn, indeed, we have for a moment and in a certain degree a mood in which our promptings and aversions come near to being such as are proper to men. But something is sure to happen before the morning is over, by which these better feelings are either checked or perhaps utterly destroyed. And in the end, when they have been checked again and again, the night air is no longer able to preserve them, and soon our feelings are as near as may be to those of beasts and birds; so that any one might make the same mistake about us as about the mountain, and think that there was never any good in us from the very start. Yet assuredly our present state of feeling is not what we began with. Truly,[1]

"If rightly tended, no creature but thrives;
If left untended, no creature but pines away."

[1] See Add. Notes on Chapter I.

The Way and its Power

Confucius said:

> "Hold fast to it and you can keep it,
> Let go, and it will stray.
> For its comings and goings it has no time nor tide;
> None knows where it will bide."

Surely it was of the feelings[1] that he was speaking?'

I have started with these two passages because they seem to me to represent, typically and forcibly, two contrasting attitudes towards life, and what I want to give some idea of in this introduction is the interplay of these two attitudes and the gradual victory[2] of the second over the first. The passage from the *Book of History* belongs to what has been called the pre-moral phase of society. All societies of which we know passed through such a stage. All the 'moral' words (virtue, righteousness, kindness, nobility), unless they are recent formations, had quite other meanings earlier in their history. 'Moral' itself of course simply meant 'customary', as did also the Greek *dikaios* (righteous). *Virtus* originally meant the inherent power in a person or thing; which is very different from what we mean by virtue. *Nobilis* meant belonging to a particular class of society. *Gentilis* did not mean 'gentle', but belonging to a certain group of families. Pre-moral is merely a negative name. It is more difficult to find a positive one, but I have got into the habit of thinking about this phase

[1] i.e. the innate good feelings.
[2] The essence of the 'moral' attitude is that it regards good as an end in itself, apart from rewards either immediate or contingent. Such a view has of course never been held in a pure and undiluted form save by small minorities. Christianity itself, with its deferred rewards, and Buddhism too, both represent a compromise.

Introduction

of society as the 'auguristic-sacrificial'; for its tendency is to make thought centre largely round the twin occupations of augury and sacrifice. These however are merely means towards a further end, the maintenance of communication between Heaven and Earth. It is easy enough to see what Earth means. It means the people who dwell on earth. Now Heaven too (in China, at any rate) is a collective term and means the people who dwell in Heaven, just as the House of Lords frequently means the people who sit in that House. These 'people in Heaven' are the ancestors (*ti*) and they are ruled over by the 'supreme ancestor' (*shang ti*), first of the ancestral line. They know the whole past of the tribe and therefore can calculate its whole future; by means of augury it is possible to use their knowledge. They live in Heaven; thence comes the weather, which is 'Heaven's mood', and it is wise to share with them all such things as depend for their growth on Heaven's good mood.

Into this outlook there enters no notion of actions or feelings that are good in themselves. People of the tenth century B.C. would assuredly have been at a complete loss to understand what Mencius (in the second half of the third century B.C.) meant by his passionate and moving plea for the theory that 'man is by nature good'. Goodness, to these early people, meant obtaining lucky omens, keeping up the sacrifices (and unless the omens were favourable no sacrifice could be carried out); goodness meant conformity to the way of Heaven, that is to say, to the way of the Ancestors collectively; it meant the possession of the 'power' (*tê*) that this conformity brings. What possible meaning could it have to say that man is 'born good'?

The Way and its Power

In order to give an idea of the contrast between these two opposing phases of thought, I have chosen two characteristic passages. I want now to go back and examine each of these phases rather more closely. The world of omens and magic ritual to which the Honan oracle-bones[1] and the *Book of Changes*[2] introduce us is one with which we are already familiar in Babylonia.[3] Things that happen are divided into two classes: the things that man does on purpose and the things that 'happen of themselves'. All the latter class of things (not only in ancient but also in modern China, among the peasants, as indeed among the remoter rural populations all over the world) is ominous. 'Feelings' in different parts of the body,[4] stumbling, twitching, itching, sneezing, buzzing in the ears, trembling in the eyelids, unaccountable movements of pliant objects held in the hand—all are 'communications' from Heaven, from the Ancestors. Then there is, apart from the class of omens connected with one's own person, the whole rich category of outside omens—signs given by birds, insects, animals, thunder and lightning, the stars.[5]

[1] The best general account of these is given by W. Perceval Yetts, *Journal of the Royal Asiatic Society*, July, 1933, pp. 657-685. The inscriptions, only a small proportion of which have been interpreted, date from the 12th and 11th centuries B.C. They are the oldest Chinese writing which survives.

[2] See my article in the *Bulletin of the Museum of Far Eastern Antiquities*, Stockholm, No. 5.

[3] See Jastrow, *Religion Babyloniens und Assyriens*.

[4] *Changes* §31.

[5] The formation of the Chinese script and the evidence of early literature suggest that astrology, i.e. the linking of human fate to the motions of the stars, came comparatively late and was due to foreign influence. See Maspero, *La Chine Antique*, p. 615.

22

Introduction

Birds are, of course, the intermediaries between heaven and earth. But they are also the great voyagers and know what is happening to human travellers in distant parts. It is above all the wild-goose that in the *Book of Changes*, in the *Odes* and all through the subsequent course of Chinese literature, is appealed to for omens concerning the absent. Of insects the most informative is the ant (*i*) because of its 'morality' (*i*) in the primitive sense of the word—its 'orderliness' in corporate movement, and also because of its uncanny foreknowledge of weather conditions.[1] Of animals the most ominous is the swine. Indeed a large number of the Chinese characters denoting movement ('to drive out', 'to follow', 'to retreat') contain the element 'swine'. A herd of swine with white trotters crossing a stream is a portent of heavy rain.[2]

Of all elements in ritual 'none is more important than sacrifice'.[3] Constantly in early Chinese literature the maintenance of offerings to the ancestors is represented as the ultimate aim of all social institutions. A country that is unable to keep up these offerings has lost its existence. The importance of sacrifice in early China is again reflected both in the written characters and in the language. Hundreds of common words and characters in everyday use at the present time owe their origin to sacrifice and the rituals connected with it. I will give only one example. The word now written 'heart' *plus* 'blood' originally meant to draw blood from a sacrificial animal. If it bled freely, this meant that the ancestors accepted the sacrifice.

[1] If the ants come up out of their holes at Christmas there will be no further snowfall till Epiphany, say the Alpine peasants.
[2] *Odes* No. 232.   [3] *Li Chi*, 25, beginning. The references are to the *Li Chi Chi Shuo* arrangement, in 49 books.

Hence, by metaphor, if one's sufferings drew a response from other people, these people were said to 'bleed' for one, in fact, to 'sympathize', which is the only meaning that the word now has. There were a host of other rituals, the nature of which is no longer clear. The Oracle Bones teem with names of rites which have not been identified.[1]

About 400 B.C.[2] or perhaps earlier a changed attitude towards sacrifice and divination begins to appear; as shown by arguments in the *Tso Chuan*,[3] put into the mouths of people who lived in very early days, but certainly reflecting a much later state of feelings: the object of sacrifice is to prove to the ancestors that their descendants are prospering. Until practical steps have been taken to make the people prosper, there should be no sacrifices. Man, it is argued comes first, the spirits second; just as 'man is near, but heaven far away'. The ritualists of the Confucian school, perhaps about 300 B.C. or earlier, go a great deal further. 'Sacrifice', says the *Li Chi*,[4] 'is not something that comes from outside. It is something that comes from inside, being born in our hearts (feelings); when the heart is uneasy, we support it with ritual.' 'Sacrifice', says Hsün Tzŭ[5] (quoting from an earlier document),

---

[1] I have dealt with the *bêng* ceremony, by means of which luck was 'stabilized' in my paper on the *Book of Changes*. See above, p. 22. I could now add fresh evidence on the subject.

[2] Certain passages in the *Analects* seem to regard sacrifice as only of subjective importance, e.g. III, 12.

[3] Duke Huan, 6th year; Duke Chao, 18th year.

[4] Ch. 25.

[5] *P'ien* 19, end. c.f. *Kuan Tzŭ*, 2: 'neither sacrifice nor the offering of tablets of jade and discs of jade are in themselves enough to content the spirits of the dead'.

Introduction

'is a state of mind in which our thoughts turn with longing (towards Heaven, the Ancestors). It is the supreme expression of loyalty, love and respect. It is the climax of all those ritual prescriptions which we embody in patterned (*wên*) behaviour. Only a Sage can understand its real significance. It is for gentlemen and nobles quietly to carry out, for officers of state to protect it, for the common people to make it part of their common usage. The nobles know well enough that it belongs to the way of man. Only common people regard it as a service rendered to spirits of the dead.'

The attitude towards divination underwent a similar change. 'If the ruler', says *Kuan Tzŭ*,[1] 'relies on the tortoise and the divining-stalks, if he is partial to the use of shamans[2] and magicians, the result will merely be that ghosts and spirits will get into the habit of "entering into" people.' That it is not enough to receive a good omen, that one must annex it to oneself by some further ritual is a view that was certainly held in ancient China; and I imagine that parallels could be found elsewhere. Gradually, however, as we advance into the moralistic period, we find a new theory being developed: omens mean quite different things according to whether they appear to good or to bad people. 'I have heard that, though good omens are the forerunners of heavenly blessings, if one sees a good omen and then acts wickedly, the blessings will not come. So too bad omens are the forerunners of disaster. But if one sees a bad omen and acts

---

[1] *P'ien* 3.

[2] *Wu*, who performed ecstatic dances, being 'possessed' by the spirits of the dead.

25

virtuously, no disaster will ensue.'[1] To give these words
the requisite authority they are, in accordance with an
invariable Chinese practice, put into the mouth of an
ancient worthy—the founder of the Shang dynasty whom
we may place somewhere about the 17th century B.C.
Han Fei Tzŭ,[2] in the great litany which enumerates the
forty-seven causes that can bring a state to decay says: 'If
a kingdom use hours and days (i.e. believes in lucky and
unlucky times), if it serves ghosts and spirits, if it puts
trust in divination by the tortoise or by the yarrow-stalks
and loves sacrifices and intercessions it will surely decay.'

I have spoken of the shaman being 'possessed' by spirits.
But there was another functionary, far more regularly connected with Chinese ritual, in whom the Ancestors, the
'royal guests' at the sacrificial banquet, habitually took
their abode. This was the *shih*, the medium (literally,
'corpse') who sitting silent and composed, represented the
ancestor to whom the sacrifice was made, or at funerals
played the role of the dead man. Now this sort of
'medium' does not, so far as I know, form part, in other
ancient civilizations, of the ritual pattern connected with
sacrifice; and it is possible that this is a case of the exten-
sion of funeral ritual to the sacrificial cult of the dead.
But there is no doubt about the antiquity of the custom.
The medium appears not only in the ritual-books, which
are records not so much of actual practice as of contro-
versies between rival schools of ritualistic theoreticians,
but also in the *Book of Odes*, one of the most unquestion-

[1] *Lü Shih Ch'un Ch'iu*, P'ien 29, beginning. There is a good
translation of *Lü Shih Ch'un Ch'iu* by Richard Wilhelm. Jena. 1928.
[2] P'ien 15. Written in the 3rd century B.C.

26

Introduction

ably ancient of Chinese sources. The great Chu Hsi, in
the 12th century A.D., even went so far as to say that a
medium was used in all sacrifices whether to nature-
spirits or to ancestors;[1] though he was puzzled as to
whether one was ever used in sacrificing to Heaven-and-
Earth.[2] The early Chinese, then, were accustomed to the
idea of spirits entering into human beings, and in the
moralistic period the idea began to grow up that such
spirits, if their new abode were made sufficiently attract-
ive, might be induced to stay in it permanently, or at least
during periods other than those of sacrificial ritual. Hence
grew up the idea of 'soul', of a god or spirit more or less
permanently dwelling inside an individual. Several words
competed for this new meaning: One of them was T'ien,
'Heaven', 'The Abode of the Ancestors'. For example,
'Restrict your appetites and needs, abandon knowledge
and scheming, put away all crafty calculations; let your
thoughts wander in the abode of the Inexhaustible, set
your heart upon the path of that which is so-of-itself, do
this and your "heaven" shall be safe from destruction.'[3]
Or the parallel passage in Chuang Tzŭ:[4] 'Wander to where
the ten thousand things both begin and end, unify your
nature, foster your life-breath, concentrate your "power"[5]
till it is one with the force that created all things after
their kind—do this, and your "heaven" shall maintain its
integrity.'

[1] Quoted in I Li I Su, XXXIV, 14.
[2] His hesitation was well justified, for the conception of Heaven-
and-Earth as a kind of joint, twin deity is a late one. For a further
discussion of the shih (medium) see additional notes.
[3] Lü Shih Ch'un Ch'iu, P'ien 14.
[4] XIX. 2.   [5] See below, p. 31.

27

The Way and its Power

Another word that often comes near to meaning 'soul' is _ch'i,_ the word that I have translated 'life-breath' in the passage just quoted. Originally it means a vapour that rises out of anything. As written to-day it means literally 'the vapour that rises from cooked grain'. The weather is heaven's _ch'i;_ the essences (or 'spirits' as we often say) of herbs and drugs are their _ch'i. Ch'i_ is the air. Man receives a portion of it at birth, and this is his life-breath, the source of energy, the motive-power of the senses. Another word often translated soul is _hun,_ the 'cloud' that comes out of the mouth on frosty mornings. When the dualist theory became dominant in China and everything had to be classified in pairs of male and female, the _hun_ became the male soul, mounting to heaven when a man died; while _p'o,_ which originally meant the semen,[1] becomes the female soul, which lodges in the tomb. The word which however in the end won the day, and may be said to be, from the beginning of the Christian era onwards, the most ordinary word for soul, is _shên._ It comes from a root meaning 'to stretch'. The spirits of the dead were called 'stretchers' because they had the power to cause easy parturition, to stretch the womb. The word for thunder was written in early times with the same character as _shên;_ for thunder was, in early times, as our own language attests,[2] considered to be the stretcher _par excellence._[3]

The spirits of the dead, then, honourably called

[1] This meaning was retained by the word, in non-philosophic parlance, till modern times. See the story about hanged men in _Pên Ts'ao Kang Mu_ LII (16th century).

[2] 'Thunder' is akin to Latin _tonitrus,_ which, in turn, is cognate to τόνος, 'stretched string', and τείνειν, 'to stretch'.

[3] I feel now (1948) some doubt about these etymologies.

28

'stretchers' (*shên*), are 'nourished' by sacrifices and offerings, and at the time of the sacrifice they enter into the medium, but only as guests. The idea that a *shên* could be a permanent part of a living person's inner equipment does not occur, I think, till the 3rd century B.C.[1] Even so, we are still far from the complete conception of the soul as a kind of twin to the body. To begin with, the word in its subjective sense is used almost exclusively in connection with sages and rulers, and it is not at all clear that ordinary people were supposed to possess a *shên*.[2] 'If the monarch loses his *shên*', says *Han Fei Tzŭ*, 'the tigers[3] will soon be on his tracks.'[4]

'The Sages of old', says the *Lü Shih Ch'un Ch'iu*,[5] meaning of course legendary ancient rulers like Yao and Shun, 'did not injure their souls by petty feelings about private matters; they sat quietly and waited.'

I have still a number of other words to discuss. The reader will perhaps at this point begin to wonder whether I have lost sight of my original purpose in writing this introductory essay and have, owing to a predisposition towards philology, forgotten Chinese thought and slipped into writing a treatise on the Chinese language. I can only say that I see no other way of studying the history of thought except by first studying the history of words, and such a study would seem to me equally necessary if I were dealing with the Greeks, the Romans, the Egyptians, the

[1] Legge once gives *shên* a subjective sense in the *Tso Chuan* (p. 382), but this is clearly a mistranslation. There is no example in *Mencius*.

[2] In *Han Fei*, P'ien 20, an ordinary philosopher is spoken of as 'wearing out his soul'. But there are reasons for supposing that this section is late. cf. Appendix VI.

[3] i.e. his political opponents.

[4] *Han Fei*, P'ien 8.   [5] P'ien 119

Hebrews, or any other people. For example, in reading the Bible, whether for edification or literary pleasure, we do not trouble to enquire whether abstract words like 'righteousness' mean the same thing all through the Old Testament, or whether (as I should certainly expect) they mean something quite different in the more primitive parts of the Pentateuch from what they mean in the later prophets. Nor do we pause to ask what the different words rendered by 'soul', 'spirit' and so on really meant to the people who used them. But anyone studying the history of Hebrew thought would be bound to ask himself these questions, and I cannot think that it is superfluous to ask them with regard to Chinese. I will confine myself here, however, to three further words, all of which occur frequently in the *Tao Tê Ching*. The first is the word *tao* itself. It means a road, path, way; and hence, the way in which one does something; method, principle, doctrine. The Way of Heaven, for example, is ruthless; when autumn comes 'no leaf is spared because of its beauty, no flower because of its fragrance'. The Way of Man means, among other things, procreation; and eunuchs are said to be 'far from the Way of Man'. *Chu Tao* is 'the way to be a monarch', i.e. the art of ruling. Each school of philosophy had its *tao*, its doctrine of the way in which life should be ordered. Finally in a particular school of philosophy whose followers ultimately came to be called Taoists, *tao* meant 'the way the universe works'; and ultimately, something very like God, in the more abstract and philosophical sense of that term.

Now it so happens that all the meaning-extensions of this word *tao* (even including the last: 'I am the Way') also

Introduction

exist in European languages, so that Western scholars have had no difficulty in understanding it. The same cannot be said of another, equally important term, *tê*. It is usually translated 'virtue', and this often seems to work quite well; though where the word occurs in early, pre-moralistic texts such a translation is in reality quite false. But if we study the usage of the word carefully we find that *tê* can be bad as well as good. What is a 'bad virtue'? Clearly 'virtue' is not a satisfactory equivalent. Indeed, on examining the history of the word we find that it means something much more like the Indian *karma*, save that the fruits of *tê* are generally manifested here and now; whereas *karma* is bound up with a theory of transmigration, and its effects are usually not seen in this life, but in a subsequent incarnation. *Tê* is anything that happens to one or that one does of a kind indicating that, as a consequence, one is going to meet with good or bad luck. It means, so to speak, the stock of credit (or the deficit) that at any given moment a man has at the bank of fortune. Such a stock is of course built up partly by the correct carrying out of ritual; but primarily by securing favourable omens; for unless the omens are favourable, no rite can be carried out at all.

But the early Chinese also regarded the planting of seeds as a *tê*. The words 'to plant' (ancient Chinese, *dhyek*) and *tê* (anciently *tek*) are cognate, and in the earliest script they share a common character.[1] Thus *tê* is bound up with the idea of potentiality. Fields planted with corn represent potential riches; the appearance of a rainbow, potential disaster; the falling of 'sweet dew', potential

[1] See Takata, *Kochūhen*, under the character *tê*.

31

peace and prosperity. Hence *tê* means a latent power, a 'virtue' inherent in something.

Only when the moralistic position was thoroughly established, that is to say, after the doctrines of Confucianism had become a State orthodoxy,[1] did *tê*, at any rate among the upper classes, come to mean what we usually mean by virtue, that is to say, conduct beautiful and admirable in itself (as a work of art is beautiful) apart from its consequences.

The last of these 'moral' words with which I propose to deal is *i*[2] 'morality', perhaps the most important of them all. '*I*' means what is right, proper, fitting, decent; what one would expect under the circumstances; what is, as we should say, 'in order'. In 542 B.C. a noble lady was burnt to death in a palace fire owing to the fact that she would not leave the house until a chaperon could be found to escort her. Such conduct, says the historian, would have been proper in the case of a young girl; but a married woman (in this case a quite elderly one) would certainly not have been blamed for acting as was 'reasonable under the circumstances' (*i*)[3]. Or again, 'To drink only as much as is necessary to fulfil the rites and not to continue the feast till it becomes a riot—that is *i*'.[4]

But in the period centring round 300 B.C. the question[5] was asked, is not the conduct that we call *i* (moral) merely

---

[1] Say, from the 1st cent. A.D. onwards; but *tê* has never entirely shed its old pre-moralistic meanings, any more than our word 'virtue' had entirely discarded the sense of 'inherent power'.

[2] Giles: Nos. 5354 and 5454, which are merely two different ways of writing the same word.

[3] *Tso Chuan*, Duke Hsiang, 30th year.

[4] *Tso Chuan*, Duke Chuang, 22nd year.   [5] *Mencius*, VI. 1. 5.

the outward expression of a feeling about what is right
and wrong, and is it not this feeling, rather than the outward manifestation of it, that we ought to call morality?
Thus just as the words for soul, spirit, etc., had begun
their career as names for outside things, and ended by
being names for parts of man's interior, psychological
equipment, so the word *i*, which at first meant little more
than sensible, reasonable conduct, came in the end to mean
something very like 'conscience'. Man, indeed, was dis-
covering that he was a much more interesting creature
than he had supposed. There dwelt inconspicuously within him a strange thing called a soul, which was of the
same nature as the venerated Ancestors in Heaven, as the
spirits of the rivers, hills and groves. There was moreover, buried in his heart, a mysterious power which, if he
would but use it, enabled him to distinguish between
these two new classes into which he now divided everything—the morally-good and the morally-bad—to discriminate with a sense as unerring as that which enabled
him to tell the sweet from the bitter, the light from the
dark. Never in the most ancestor-fearing days, when
Heaven had an eye that saw all, an ear that heard all, had
it been suggested that the whole universe lay, concentrated as it were, inside the Supreme Ancestor or any one
of the Dead Kings. Yet this was the claim that Mencius
made for common man. 'The ten thousand things', he
says, meaning the whole cosmos, 'are there complete,
inside us.'[1]

[1] For the connection of Mencius with the Ch'i school of Taoism, see
below. Such passages have of course been explained away by the Confucians. Legge, though he follows the official interpretation, does so

The Way and its Power

Man on earth, then, so far from being a pale shadow of the Ancestors, possesses within himself all the attributes that in ancient times made the cult of the Former Kings the supreme end of all tribal activity. · It was to himself, as the possessor of 'heavenliness', of 'spirit', of the mysterious sense called *i* which enabled him, without consulting yarrow-stalks or the tortoise, to discriminate between right and wrong—it was to himself that each man owed the worship and veneration that had once been accorded to Heaven, the home of the Dead Kings. And since the cult of the Ancestors was the main common activity of the State at large, it followed that the transference of this cult to the individual left the State with a sphere of action greatly limited, indeed, according to one School,[1] reduced to nil. A perfect community, these philosophers argued, implies perfect individuals. Let each man perfect himself. If the State asks from him one single act that interferes with this process of self-perfection, he should refuse, not merely on his own account, but out of regard for the community which corporately suffers in as far as one of its members is 'imperfect'. 'The men of old[2] would not have given one hair of their bodies to help the State. Nor if every one in the State (hair by hair and

with some misgiving, remarking that the passage seems 'quite mystical'.

[1] That of Yang Chu. See *Lieh Tzŭ* VII, which is however not an official account, by the Yang Chu school itself, of the master's teachings, but a late hearsay account in which the original teachings of Yang Chu are mixed up with the hedonistic doctrine which grew up in one branch of his school. The polemic references to Yang Chu in *Mencius* are mere parody.

[2] New theories were always put forward as revivals of ancient practice. See Appendix I.

34

joint by joint) had sacrificed themselves for them, would they have been willing to accept such a sacrifice. For it is only when every one in the State is whole and perfect down to the last hair and each individual attends to himself and stops thinking about benefiting the State, that the State is itself sound.'[1]

But the divine faculties of man, which make it a sacrilege to demand from him the surrender of even 'one hair from his leg', maintain a precarious existence. The *shên* (soul) is like a grandee on his travels.[2] If the inn is not well managed and tidy, he will not stay there. How, then, can the body be made a fit dwelling-place for the soul? Or if we regard the soul not as something that comes and goes but rather as a faculty fettered and impeded by the stress of daily life,[3] how can we ensure its freedom? Traditional experience concerning the behaviour of *shên*, of divinities, suggested that the first essential was abstinence and fasting. In the old sacrificial life[4] it had been regarded as useless to expect the Royal Guests (the dead kings) to descend in their spirit (*shên*) form and partake of the sacrifice, unless the sacrificer had first prepared himself by three days abstinence and fasting.[5] The term *chai* (abstinence and fasting) implied the curbing of all sensual and physical activities. The exercise, then, of any of the

[1] *Lieh Tzŭ* VII. 9.   [2] *Kuan Tzŭ*, P'ien 36, beginning.   [3] As in *Mencius*.
[4] I do not of course mean that sacrifice had totally disappeared, but only that it had lost its significance to the thinking classes.
[5] The original purpose of fasting was of course not self-purification (which is a relatively late, moralistic idea) but the desire to 'move the hearts' of the Ancestors. Carried to its logical conclusion it can include self-mutilation and self-disfigurement of all kinds. It was in the same spirit that suppliants to earthly potentates disfigured themselves, poured ashes on their heads, etc.

senses, whether of sight, smell, taste or hearing, the use of any sinew or limb, was regarded as a potential menace to the soul. If this menace were physical, if it were directly observable, we should all be sages. 'Suppose there were some sound which, when the ear heard it, was agreeable but which caused the ear afterwards to go deaf, we should take good care not to listen to it. Suppose there were some colour which, when the eye saw it, was agreeable but which caused blindness to follow, we should take good care not to look at it.'[1] Unhappily the wrong use of the senses is deleterious in a far subtler way; in as far then as government of any kind is needed, in a state where each person is privately perfecting his own inner nature, it will consist in the presence among the people of 'better people' who will tell them which physical satisfactions are dangerous and which profitable to the 'life within'. But these 'better people' (*hsien*) must not form a separate class supported by the labour of others, and so allowing themselves to be 'completed' at the expense of other people's 'incompleteness'. It was, I think, ideas of this kind that inspired the followers of Hsü Hsing, who dressed in coarse haircloth, wore hemp sandals instead of leather shoes and supported themselves by weaving mats; the people whom Mencius rebuked by quoting the saying: 'Some work with their minds, others with their bodies. Those who work with the mind rule; those who work with the body are ruled. Those who are ruled feed their rulers; those who rule, feed upon those they rule.' 'Which', Mencius added, 'is accepted as common sense by every one under heaven.' Sects of this kind naturally

[1] *Lü Shih Ch'un Ch'iu*, P'ien 2.

travelled about trying to find a milieu that would be sympathetic to their doctrines. Hsü Hsing and his followers had, when interviewed by Mencius,[1] already trekked some four hundred miles. If unsuccessful in this quest they settled in some remote spot outside the sphere of governmental interference. The literature of the 3rd century B.C. is full of references to recluses, people who 'lived among rocks or in holes in the ground' and 'even if they were offered salaried employments would not accept them'.[2]

'A ruler', says *Kuan Tzŭ*,[3] 'should not listen to those who believe in people having opinions of their own and in the importance of the individual. Such teachings cause men to withdraw to quiet places and hide away in caves or on mountains, there to rail at the prevailing government, sneer at those in authority, belittle the importance of rank and emoluments, and despise all who hold official posts'. As we have seen, the real reason why such persons refused to draw official salaries and insisted on living in their own way on the fruit of their own labour was that they thought society should consist of individuals each complete in himself, and it was against their consciences to be supported by 'hairs' drawn from the suffering head of the community at large. A certain Ch'ên Chung was a scrupulous recluse of this class. He belonged to an important family in the land of Ch'i (now part of Shantung). His ancestors had held high office for many generations on end, and his elder brother administered a fief from which

[1] Actually, their views were transmitted to Mencius by an intermediary.

[2] *Han Fei Tzŭ*, 45 and 49.   [3] P'ien 65.

he received a revenue of 10,000 *chung*.[1] As it was against
Ch'ên Chung's principles to live on what he regarded as
ill-gotten gains, he left his brother's house and set up at a
remote place called Wu-ling. Here he supported himself
by making hemp-sandals, his wife twisting the hemp-
thread. Their livelihood was very precarious and on one
occasion Ch'ên had nothing to eat for three days. 'His
ears no longer heard, his eyes no longer saw.' But he knew
that on a tree by the well-side there was a plum, half eaten
by maggots. In desperation he groped his way to the spot,
gulped the plum down, and so recovered his sight and
hearing.

Once when he was staying for a while at his brother's
house someone sent the family a live goose as a present.
'What use can they suppose you could make of a cackling
thing like that?' Ch'ên Chung asked, frowning. A few
days later his mother killed the goose and not telling him
what it was gave him some for his dinner. 'I suppose you
know what it is you are eating,' said his brother, coming
into the room. 'That's cackle-cackle's flesh!' Ch'ên went
out into the courtyard and vomited.

We might be tempted to think that Ch'ên Chung was,
among his other scrupulosities, a vegetarian. But I do not
think that is the point of the story. He regarded the
goose, which was no doubt a gift from one of the tenants,

[1] A tenth of the revenue of a prime minister. The story of Ch'ên
Chung will be found in *Mencius*, III. 2. 10. He is said also to have
worked as a gardener (*Shih Chi*, 83, end). A collection of anecdotes concerning him, entitled *Wu-ling Tzŭ*, made its appearance in the 16th
century, and is in all probability the work of Hsü Wei (Wên-ch'ang),
1520-1593. The surname Ch'ên was pronounced T'ien in the Ch'i
state, and he is therefore sometimes called T'ien Chung.

Introduction

as part of his brother's ill-gotten gains; hence his dis-
approval of the arrival of 'cackle-cackle' and his nausea at
the thought of having partaken of such a dish.[1]

The Hedonists

The transference of attention from the dead to the living, from heaven to earth, was due not merely to the discovery that 'of all things Man is the most spirit-fraught
(*ling*)', but also to a doubt whether the dead, even if they
could be said in any sense to exist beyond the grave, were
conscious of what happened on earth. Mo Tzŭ[2] devotes a
chapter to the confutation of those who believe that the
dead do not 'exist' and that consequently sacrifices and
libations are a waste of time and food. 'It is no waste at
all,' replies Mo Tzŭ, 'even admitting that there are no
such things as spirits of the dead. One might call it waste
indeed, if the wine and so on were merely poured into the
gutter. But in point of fact, the members of the family
and friends in the village all get their share, so that, at
worst, sacrificing makes an excuse for bringing people
together and helps us to get on to better terms with our
neighbours.' This view of religion as a social bond (modern supporters of this theory are able to point to the
supposed etymology of the word religion—'a binding
together') is highly sophisticated. But elsewhere we find a
doubt as to the consciousness of the dead side by side with

[1] A great many stories of hermits and recluses could be cited from
Chuang Tzŭ and *Lieh Tzŭ*, but most of them are more or less in the
nature of fairy-tales.

[2] P'ien 31, which probably represents the views of the Mo school
c. 300 B.C. Mo Tzŭ has been translated into German by Alfred Forke
and (part only) into English by Y. P. Mei, 1926.

the mention of very primitive practices. In 265 B.C. the wife of the former ruler of Ch'in lay dying. She was greatly attached to a stranger from the Wei state, and gave orders that he was to be sacrificed at her funeral, in order that his spirit might escort her beyond the grave. The stranger from Wei was much upset, and a friend interviewed the dying lady on his behalf, saying: 'Do you believe that the dead are conscious?' 'I do not think they are,' she said. 'If the spirit (*shên*) immanent within you indeed knows clearly that the dead are not conscious, then what possible good can it do you, great lady, that one whom you loved in life should go with you into a state where there is no consciousness? If on the other hand the dead are conscious, a fine rage the late king will be in! "Here's the queen," he will say, "who has been hovering between life and death for months past, arriving with a man from Wei! She can't have been quite as ill all the time as she led people to suppose." ' The queen said 'How true!' and desisted.[1]

The idea that morality is merely the desire to be thought well of, and that the dead do not know what we think about them, with the natural inference that it is best to get all that we can out of life, without worrying about what sort of reputation we leave behind, is attributed to the Hedonists by *Lieh Tzŭ*:[2] the whole admiration of the world is concentrated upon four paragons, Shun, the

[1] *Chan Kuo Ts'ê*, III. 52.

[2] VII. 10, end. Shun was a culture-hero, who wore himself out ploughing and potting. The Great Yü battled against the Floods. For the Duke of Chou, see above, p. 17. Legend makes Confucius the subject of a long series of insults and persecutions, due to the un-popularity of his teaching.

Introduction

Great Yü, the Duke of Chou and Confucius; yet it would be hard to imagine sorrier objects of admiration. These men led dismal and laborious lives under the impression that they were benefiting mankind and would win its eternal praises. The praise is there; but for all the difference it makes to them they might as well be clods of earth or stumps of trees. So, for that matter, might the 'bad' kings Chieh and Chou, upon whom every sort of abuse is heaped. But they at least made the most of life while it lasted, building glorious palaces, feasting far into the night, unhampered by any scruples about seemliness or morality.

The doctrine of these hedonists was called *yang-shêng*, 'nourishing the living'[1] as opposed to nourishing the dead. What most 'nourishes life' is happiness, and what leads to happiness is the freedom to satisfy desire. The ruler's duty, then (and every Chinese philosophy is formulated not as an abstract theory but as an 'art of ruling') is to give free play to every desire, whether of the body or of the mind: 'Let the ear hear what it longs to hear, the eye see what it longs to see, the nose smell what it likes to smell, the mouth speak what it wants to speak, let the body have every comfort that it craves, let the mind do as it will. Now what the ear wants to hear is music,[2] and to deprive it of this is to cramp the sense of hearing. What the eye

[1] This was, I think the earliest sense of the term. The Confucians used it in the sense of 'nurturing the living' (i.e. one's parents), as opposed to 'nurturing the dead' (i.e. sacrifice to the ancestors). *Yang-shêng* is however often taken in the subjective sense of 'nourishing one's own life', i.e. fostering one's vital energy.

[2] The Confucians discouraged all such music as was not morally uplifting; the school of Mo Tzŭ forbade music altogether.

41

wants to see is carnal beauty; and to deprive it is to cramp the sense of sight. What the nose craves for is to have near it the fragrant plants *shu* and *lan*; and if it cannot have them, the sense of smell is cramped. What the mouth desires is to speak of what is true and what false; and if it may not speak, then knowledge is cramped. What the body desires for its comfort is warmth and good food. Thwart its attainment of these, and you cramp what is natural and essential to man. What the mind wants is the liberty to stray whither it will, and if it has not this freedom, the very nature of man is cramped and thwarted. Tyrants and oppressors cramp us in every one of these ways. Let us depose them, and wait happily for death to come.'[1]

Such views must have gained considerable currency, for we find them ranged alongside of the other principal doctrines of the day (such as those of Kung-sun Lung, the pacificist, and Mo Tzŭ) in a denunciation of doctrines prejudicial to good government. 'A ruler of men should on no account encourage those who preach the doctrine of "perfecting the individual life". For should he do so, then all his ministers will apply themselves with alacrity to perfecting their lives, which is the same thing as nurturing their lives. And what is this "life-nurturing"? It consists in feasting, music and love. That is the way that the followers of this doctrine set about "nurturing life". To encourage them is to open up the way to licence and

[1] *Lieh Tzŭ* VII. 5. The same sentiments are attributed to the robber Chê by *Chuang Tzŭ* XXIX. 1, end, and by *Hsün Tzŭ* to Tzŭ Mou, prince of Wei, who wrote a book which unfortunately has not survived.

depravity, to abolish the separation of the sexes, and in fact to return to the condition of wild beasts.'[1]

Quietism

There was another sect that, though its way of life was exactly the opposite of that commended by the Hedonists, met with equally severe condemnation. *Han Fei Tzŭ*[2] speaks of people who 'walk apart from the crowd, priding themselves on being different from other men. They preach the doctrine of Quietism, but their exposition of it is couched in baffling and mysterious terms. I submit to your Majesty[3] that this Quietness is of no practical value to any one and that the language in which it is couched is not founded on any real principle . . . I submit that man's duty in life is to serve his prince and nourish his parents, neither of which things can be done by Quietness. I further submit that it is man's duty, in all that he teaches, to promote loyalty and good faith and the Legal Constitution. This cannot be done in terms that are vague and mysterious. The doctrine of the Quietists is a false one, likely to lead the people astray'.

How did this doctrine arise? We have seen the gradual inward-turning of Chinese thought, its preoccupation with self and the perfection of self. We have seen how out of the ritual preparation of the sacrificer for the reception of the descending spirit grew the idea of a cleansing of the heart which should make it a fit home for the soul.

---

[1] *Kuan Tzŭ*, 65. *Kuan Tzŭ* like *Lieh Tzŭ* identifies the 'perfecters of the individual life' with the Hedonists. It is clear that at any rate in popular imagination the Hedonists were an offshoot of the school of Yang Chu.

[2] P'ien 51.   [3] The king of Ch'in.

The Way and its Power

Such cleansing consisted above all in a 'stilling' of outward activities, of appetites and emotions; but also in a 'returning'; for the soul was looked upon as having become as it were silted up by successive deposits of daily toil and perturbation, and the business of the 'self-perfecter' was to work his way back through these layers till 'man as he was meant to be' was reached. Through this 'stillness', this complete cessation of outside impressions, and through the withdrawal of the senses to an entirely interior point of focus, arose the species of self-hypnosis which in China is called *Tso-wang*, 'sitting with blank mind', in India *Yoga*, *dhyāna* and other names; in Japan, Zen. A definite technique was invented[1] for producing this state of trance. The main feature of this technique was, as in India, breath-manipulation—the breathing must be soft and light as that of an infant, or, as later Quietists said, of a child in the womb. There were also strange exercises of the limbs, stretchings and postures[2] much like the *āsanas* connected with Indian *yoga*; but some Quietists regarded these as too physical and concrete a method for the attainment of a spiritual end.

The process of Quietism, then, consisted in a travelling back through the successive layers of consciousness to the point when one arrived at Pure Consciousness, where one no longer saw 'things perceived', but 'that whereby we perceive'. For never to have known 'that whereby we know' is to cast away a treasure that is ours.[3] Soon on the 'way back' one comes to the point where language, created

---

[1] Or borrowed. See Appendix II.   [2] *Chuang Tzŭ*, XV. 1.
[3] *Lü Shih Ch'un Ch'iu*, 23.

44

Introduction

to meet the demands of ordinary, upper consciousness, no longer applies. The adept who has reached this point has learnt, as the Quietists expressed it in their own secret language, 'to get into the bird-cage without setting the birds off singing'.[1]

Here a question arises, which is indeed one which Quietists have been called upon to answer in diverse parts of the world and at many widely separated periods of history. Granted that consciousness can actually be modified by *yoga*, self-hypnotism, Zen, Quietness or whatever else one chooses to call it, what evidence is there that the new consciousness has any advantage over the old? The Quietist, whether Chinese, Indian, German or Spanish, has always made the same reply: by such practices three things are attained, truth, happiness and power.

From the theoretical point of view there is of course no reason to believe that the statements of Tao are truer than those of ordinary knowledge; no more reason, in fact, than to believe that the music we hear when our radio is adjusted to 360 is any 'truer' than the music we hear when it is adjusted to 1600. But in actual practice the visions of the Quietist do not present themselves to him merely as more or less agreeable alternatives to everyday existence. They are accompanied by a sense of finality, by a feeling that 'all the problems which all the schools of philosophers under Heaven cannot settle this way or that have been settled this way or that'.[2] Moreover, the state to which the Quietist attains is not merely pleasurable

[1] *Chuang Tzŭ*, IV. 1. Pun on *fan*=(1) bird-cage (2) return, and on *ming*=(1) sing (2) name.

[2] *Chuang Tzŭ* XVIII. 1, end. *T'ien-hsia* ('under Heaven') means the various schools of philosophy.

45

The Way and its Power

rather than painful. It is 'absolute joy',[1] utterly transcending any form of earthly enjoyment. And finally, it gives as the Indians say *siddhi*, as the Chinese say *tê*, a power over the outside world undreamt of by those who pit themselves against matter while still in its thralls. Nor is this aspect of Quietism confined, as is sometimes supposed, to its eastern branches. 'Sin trabajo sujetaràs las gentes y te serviràn las cosas,' says St. John of the Cross in his Aphorisms, 'si te olvidares de ellas y de ti mismo.'[2] It is this last claim of Quietism—the belief that the practicant becomes possessed not merely of a power over living things (which we should call hypnotism) but also of a power to move and transform matter—that the world has been least disposed to accept. 'Try it (*yung chih*) and find out for yourself,' has been the Quietist's usual answer to the challenge 'show us, and we will believe'.

We know that many different schools of Quietism existed in China in the fourth and third centuries before Christ. Of their literature only a small part survives.[3] Earliest in date was what I shall call the School of Ch'i. Its doctrine was called *hsin shu* 'The Art of the Mind'.[4] By 'mind' is meant not the brain or the heart, but 'a mind within the mind' that bears to the economy of man the

[1] cf. ibidem, the whole chapter.

[2] Literally 'without labour you shall subject the peoples and things shall be subject to you, if you forget both them and yourself.'

[3] Perhaps more than we think; for it is by no means certain that *Chuang Tzŭ* does not contain teachings of several different schools. Thus it seems very probable that Chapter II represents the teaching T'ien P'ien.

[4] *Hsin* means 'heart' and 'mind'. In this system it is regarded as the repository of perceptions and knowledge, and therefore 'mind' seems more appropriate.

46

Introduction

same relation as the sun bears to the sky.[1] It is the ruler of the body, whose component parts are its ministers.[2] It must remain serene and immovable like a monarch upon his throne. It is a *shên*, a divinity, that will only take up its abode where all is garnished and swept.[3] The place that man prepares for it is called its temple (*kung*). 'Throw open the gates, put self aside, bide in silence, and the radiance of the spirit shall come in and make its home.'[4] And a little later: 'Only where all is clean will the spirit abide. All men desire to know, but they do not enquire into that whereby one knows.' And again: 'What a man desires to know is *that* (i.e. the external world). But his means of knowing is *this* (i.e. himself). How can he know *that*? Only by the perfection of *this*.'

Closely associated with the 'art of the mind' is the art of nurturing the *ch'i*,[5] the life-spirit. Fear, pettiness, meanness—all those qualities that pollute the 'temple of the mind'—are due to a shrinkage of the life-spirit. The valiant, the magnanimous, the strong of will are those whose *ch'i* pervades the whole body, down to the very toes and finger-tips.[6] A great well of energy must be stored within, 'a fountain that never dries',[7] giving

[1] *Kuan Tzŭ*, P'ien 12, beginning. *Kuan Tzŭ* merely uses fragments of Taoist texts as a mystic background for opportunist teaching.

[2] *Kuan Tzŭ*, P'ien 36, beginning.

[3] The fact that the *shên* is here in a transitional state, half outside divinity, half a 'soul' makes me think that this system is earlier than that of the better-known Taoists, to whom Tao was never a thing that came from outside.

[4] Ibidem, P'ien 36.

[5] See above p. 28. *Ch'i* may always be translated breath, if we add the proviso that to the Chinese 'breath' was a kind of soul.

[6] *Kuan Tzŭ*, 49 end.   [7] *Ibidem*, 37 end.

strength and firmness to every sinew and joint. 'Store it within; make of it a well-spring, flood-like,[1] even and level. Make of it a very store-pool of *ch'i*.

Never till that pool runs dry shall the Four Limbs fail;
Nor till the well is exhausted shall the traffic of the
    Nine Apertures cease.
Thereby[2] shall you be enabled to explore Heaven and
    Earth,
Reach the Four Oceans that bound the world;
Within, have no thoughts that perplex,
Without, suffer no evil or calamity.
Inside, the mind shall be whole;
Whole too the bodily frame.'

All this is the work of the life-breath (*ling-ch'i*) that is within the 'mind'. For it can 'come and go where it will. Be so small that nothing could go inside it; so large that nothing exists beyond it. He alone loses it who harms it by perturbation'.

What is the nature of the perturbations that cause the loss of this 'mind within the mind?' These are defined as 'grief and joy, delight and anger, desire and greed for gain. Put all these away, and your mind ("heart" would fit this particular context better) will return to its purity. For such is the mind that only peace and stillness are good for it. Do not fret, do not let yourself be perturbed and the Accord[3] will come unsought. It is close at hand,

[1] *Kuan Tzǔ*, 49 end. This is the famous *hao-jan chih ch'i* of *Mencius*.

[2] By an accumulation of *ch'i*. I see no reason to doubt that the passages here quoted refer, in a cryptic way, to practises of breath-manipulation such as those described in Appendix III.

[3] Harmony between the mind and the universe, which gives power over outside things.

Introduction

stands indeed at our very side; yet is intangible, a thing
that by reaching for cannot be got. Remote it seems as
the furthest limits of the Infinite. Yet it is not far off;
every day we use its power. For Tao (i.e. the Way of the
Vital Spirit) fills our whole frames, yet man cannot keep
track of it. It goes, yet has not departed. It comes, yet
is not here. It is muted, makes no note that can be heard,
yet of a sudden we find that it is there in the mind. It is
dim and dark, showing no outward form, yet in a great
stream it flowed into us at our birth'.[1]

The branch of Confucianism founded by Mencius was
profoundly influenced by the Ch'i-country Taoism which
centred round the Art of the Mind and the tending of
the Vital Spirit. In this there is nothing surprising, for
Mencius spent much of his life in the country of Ch'i,
now part of Shantung. Indeed, the passages in which
Mencius deals with the acquisition of the Unmoved Mind
and with the use of man's 'well-spring' of natal breath
are unintelligible unless we relate them to the much fuller
exposition of the same theories in *Kuan Tzŭ*. Mencius,
as we know, learnt the art of maintaining an 'unmoved
mind' at the age of forty,[2] that is to say on his arrival in
the country of Ch'i, which happened about 330 B.C.
When asked about the method that he employed, he
replied[3] that he had cultivated the art of using his 'flood-
like breath-spirit', obviously an allusion to the system
described by *Kuan Tzŭ*. Mencius however gives his own
turn to this doctrine. With him the 'flood-like spirit' is

[1] Ibidem, 49 beginning.   [2] *Mencius* II. 1. 2.
[3] The 'I understand words' that precedes this, belongs to par. 17,
which deals with quite a different topic and has crept in here by
mistake.

49

something that is produced cumulatively by the constant exercise of moral sense (*i*). But it can only come into existence as an accessory of such exercise. Its growth cannot be aided by any special discipline or régime. It is clear that Mencius is here combatting the ideas of the *yoga*-practitioners who performed particular exercises in order to 'expel the old (i.e. the used breath-spirit) and draw in the new'. Those who try to force the growth of the spirit by means other than the possession of a tranquil conscience he compares to the foolish man of Sung who, grieved that his crops came up so slowly, tried to help them by pulling at the stalks.[1]

Taoism

In the Ch'i system of Quietism the central conception is that of the 'mind within the mind', the sanctuary (*kung*) of the spirit. *Tao* is the way that those must walk who would 'achieve without doing'. But *tao* is not only a means, a doctrine, a principle. It is the ultimate reality in which all attributes are united, 'it is heavy as a stone, light as a feather'; it is the unity underlying plurality. 'It is that by losing of which men die; by getting of which men live. Whatever is done without it, fails; whatever is done by means of it, succeeds. It has neither root nor

[1] The traditional interpretation of the psychological parts of *Mencius* (accepted by all his translators) is an attempt not to find out what Mencius actually meant but to gloss the text in such a way as to bring it into conformity with current Confucianism. Fortunately the Quietist system that Mencius grafted on to his own theory of the instinctive moral-sense is represented (not completely but in a far more explicit form) in *Kuan Tzŭ*. I hope to deal with this question in a subsequent book of essays on Chinese philosophy.

stalk, leaf nor flower. Yet upon it depends the generation and the growth of the ten thousand things, each after its kind.'[1]

The Quietists who developed this idea of Tao as the unchanging unity underlying a shifting plurality, and at the same time the impetus giving rise to every form of life and motion, were called Taoists. The ideas of other Quietists are only known to us indirectly, through writers such as 'Kuan Tzŭ' and Mencius having utilized or adopted them. With the Taoists the case is quite different. We have in two series called *Chuang Tzŭ* and *Lieh Tzŭ* a large corpus of actual Taoist works. These works clearly do not all belong to the same branch of Taoism. Some of them have been greatly affected by the metaphysical theories of the Dualists, who attributed the whole constitution of the universe to the interaction of two opposing principles, *yin* and *yang*.[2] But other parts of the Taoist corpus show no such influence, and I do not think that this dualist conception is native to Taoism. I will try in the following pages to give some idea of the conceptions that seem to me fundamental in Taoism and that are, so far as we can judge, common ground in the various Taoist schools.

The first great principle of Taoism is the relativity of all attributes. Nothing is in itself either long or short. If we call a thing long, we merely mean longer than something else that we take as a standard. What we take as our standard depends upon what we are used to, upon the general scale of size to which we belong. The fact that we endow our standard with absoluteness and objectivity, that we say 'No one could regard this as anything but

[1] *Kuan Tzŭ*, 49.   [2] See Appendix II.

51

long!' is merely due to lack of imagination. There are birds that fly hundreds of miles without stopping. Someone mentioned this to the cicada and the wren,[1] who agreed that such a thing was out of the question. 'You and I know very well', they said, 'that the furthest one can ever get by the most tremendous effort is that elm there; and even this we can't be sure of doing every time. Often we find ourselves sinking back to earth, and have to give up the attempt as hopeless. All these stories about flying hundreds of miles at a stretch are pure nonsense.'

To those, then, who have rather more imagination than the cicada and the wren, all attributes whatsoever, whether they imply colour, height, beauty, ugliness, goodness, badness—any quality that can be thought of—are relative. And this applies, clearly, not only to the long and short, the high and low, but also to the 'inside' and 'outside'. The earlier Quietists regarded the soul as something that came from outside to dwell in the body. But to the Taoists, Tao was something that was at the same time within and without; for in Tao all opposites are blended, all contrasts harmonized.

Why did confidence in the absoluteness of any of the qualities that we attribute to things outside ourselves break down in China towards the end of the 4th century? Owing, I think, to rapidly increasing knowledge of what went on in the world outside China. Quite apart from the changes in material culture (use of iron, knowledge of asbestos, use of cavalry in war and adoption of non-Chinese dress in connection with it, familiarity with new forms of disposal of the dead) which these contacts

[1] *Chuang Tzŭ* I. 8.

brought, the Chinese were beginning to regard the world they knew merely as a grain in the Great Barn.[1]

There was no end to the wonders that this great storehouse might produce. The danger was that in face of these marvels one might, through mere bigotry and smallmindedness, adopt the attitude of the cicada and the wren. It was safer to believe everything, even that in the mountains of some remote country there dwelt mysterious beings who nourished themselves solely on air and dew, yet by the concentration of their spirit (*shên*) acquired the power to preserve flocks and herds from pest and cause the crops to grow.[2] A different standard for fasting had indeed been set since the time when Ch'ên Chung[3] collapsed after being three days without food!

The main controversy of Chinese philosophy in the 4th century B.C. had centred round the rival claims of life and death, of the Ancestors as against the living 'sons and grandsons'. To the Taoist such debates were meaningless. Looked at from Anywhere, the world is full of insecurities and contradictions; looked at from Nowhere, it is a changeless, uniform whole. In this identity of opposites all antinomies, not merely high and low, long and short, but life and death themselves merge.

'When Chuang Tzŭ's wife died, the logician Hui Tzŭ came to the house to join in the rites of mourning. To his astonishment he found Chuang Tzŭ sitting with an inverted bowl on his knees, drumming upon it and singing a song.[4] After all,' said Hui Tzŭ, 'she lived with you,

[1] *Chuang Tzŭ* XVII. 1.   [2] *Chuang Tzŭ* I. 4.
[3] See above.
[4] Both his attitude and his occupation were the reverse of what the rites of mourning demand:

53

brought up your children, grew old along with you. That you should not mourn for her is bad enough; but to let your friends find you drumming and singing—that is really going too far!' 'You misjudge me,' said Chuang Tzŭ. 'When she died, I was in despair, as any man well might be. But soon, pondering on what had happened, I told myself that in death no strange new fate befalls us. In the beginning we lack not life only, but form. Not form only, but spirit. We are blent in the one great featureless, indistinguishable mass. Then a time came when the mass evolved spirit, spirit evolved form, form evolved life. And now life in its turn has evolved death. For not nature only but man's being has its seasons, its sequence of spring and autumn, summer and winter. If someone is tired and has gone to lie down, we do not pursue him with shouting and bawling. She whom I have lost has lain down to sleep for a while in the Great Inner Room. To break in upon her rest with the noise of lamentation would but show that I knew nothing of nature's Sovereign Law.'[1]

This attitude towards death, exemplified again and again in Chuang Tzŭ, is but part of a general attitude towards the universal laws of nature, which is one not merely of resignation nor even of acquiescence, but a lyrical, almost ecstatic acceptance which has inspired some of the most moving passages in Taoist literature. That we should question nature's right to make and unmake, that we should hanker after some rôle that nature did not intend us to play is not merely futile, not merely damaging to that tranquility of the 'spirit' which is the essence

[1] *Chuang Tzŭ* XVIII. 2.

of Taoism, but involves, in view of our utter helplessness, a sort of fatuity at once comic and disgraceful. If the bronze in the founder's crucible were suddenly to jump up and say 'I don't want to be a tripod, a ploughshare or a bell. I must be the sword "Without Flaw",'[1] the bronze-caster would think it was indeed reprobate metal that had found its way into his stock.[2]

To be in harmony with, not in rebellion against the fundamental laws of the universe is the first step, then, on the way to Tao. For Tao is itself the always-so, the fixed, the unconditioned, that which 'is of itself' and for no cause 'so'. In the individual it is the Uncarved Block, the consciousness on which no impression has been 'notched', in the universe it is the Primal Unity underlying apparent multiplicity. Nearest then to Tao is the infant. Mencius, in whose system Conscience, sensitiveness to right and wrong, replaces the notion of Tao, says that the 'morally great man' is one who has kept through later years his 'infant heart'.[3] The idea is one that pervades the literature of the third century.[4] But weakness and softness in general, not only as embodied in the infant, are symbols of Tao. Such ideas as that to yield is to conquer, whereas to grasp is to lose—are indeed already inherent in the pre-

[1] Legendary heirloom of the kingdom of Wu; sharpest of mortal weapons.

[2] *Chuang Tzŭ* VI. 6.   [3] *Mencius* IV. 2. 12.

[4] e.g. *Lieh Tzŭ* I. 7, *Chuang Tzŭ* XXIII. 3. What is obviously an earlier form of the Taoist hymn used by *Chuang Tzŭ* in the passage referred to occurs in *Kuan Tzŭ* twice over (P'ien 37 and 49), and each time lacks the phrases about infancy. The idea then was probably one that did not become popular till about 300 B.C. In the early centuries of the Christian era, on the other hand, it is no longer the infant but the child in the womb that is the Taoist ideal.

moralistic phase of thought. For example by retreating from a country that one has it in one's power to lay waste, one extorts a blessing from the soil-gods and ancestral spirits of that country. Whereas by any act of aggression one ranges against one a host of unseen powers. Older too than Taoism is the idea that pride invites a fall, that the axe falls first on the tallest tree. But it was Taoism that first welded these ideas together into a system in which the unassertive, the inconspicuous, the lowly, the imperfect, the incomplete become symbols of the Primal Stuff that underlies the kaleidoscope of the apparent universe. It is as representatives of the 'imperfect' and the 'incomplete' that hunchbacks and cripples play so large a part in Taoist literature. To be perfect is to invite diminution; to climb is to invite a fall. Tao, like water, 'takes the low ground'. We have already met with the conception of the soul as a well that never runs dry. In Taoism water, as the emblem of the unassertive, and the 'low ground', as the home of water, become favourite images. The question was a controversial one; for to the early Confucians[1] the 'low ground' is the 'collecting-place of all the impurities under heaven' and hence the symbol of iniquity. *Kuan Tzŭ*[2] devotes a particularly eloquent passage to water as pattern and example to the 'ten thousand things', that is to say to everything in the universe, and to the low ground as 'dwelling-place of Tao'. It is by absorbing the water-spirit (*shui-shên*) that vegetation lives, 'that the root gets its girth, the flower its symmetries, the fruit its measure'. 'The valley-spirit',

[1] *Analects* XIX. 20.
[2] P'ien 39.

Introduction

says another Taoist work,[1] meaning what *Kuan Tzŭ* means by 'water-spirit', 'never dies. It is named the Mysterious Female,[2] and the Doorway of the Mysterious Female is the base from which Heaven and Earth sprang. It is there within us all the while; draw upon it as you will, it never runs dry.'

The valleys, then, are 'nearer to Tao' than the hills; and in the whole of creation it is the negative, passive, 'female' element alone that has access to Tao, which can only be mirrored 'in a still pool'. Quietism consists in the cultivation of this 'stillness'. In its extreme forms, consciousness continues but the functions of the outward senses are entirely suspended and the mind moves only within itself. Between this and the normal state of consciousness there are innumerable stages, and though definite *yoga*, with complete suspension of the outward senses, was certainly practised by initiate Taoists,[3] I do not think that anything more than a very relative Quiet was known to the numerous non-Taoist schools of thought that adopted Quietism as a mystical background to their teaching. There is no reason for example to suppose that Mencius's[4] 'stilling of the mind' reached an actual *samādhi*, a complete gathering in of the consciousness into itself. But it led him to make a distinction[5] between two kinds of knowledge, the one the result of mental activity, the other passive and as we should say 'intuitive'; and it is the second kind that he

[1] *The Book of the Yellow Ancestor*, quoted by *Lieh Tzŭ*, I, beginning.
[2] 'Hills are male; valleys are female.' *K'ung Tzŭ Chia Yü* 25, end. *Huai-nan Tzŭ*, Ch. IV. fol. 4.
[3] See Appendix III.
[4] Or whoever wrote the 'psychological' passages.
[5] VII. 1. 15.

57

calls 'good knowledge'. Indeed, the whole of education[1] consists, Mencius says, in recapturing intuitive faculties that in the stress of life have been allowed to go astray. With him these faculties are moral; whereas the Quiet of the Taoists produces a secondary 'virtue' (*tê*) a power 'that could shift Heaven and Earth', a transcendental knowledge in which each of the 'ten thousand things' is separately mirrored 'as the hairs of the brow and head are mirrored in a clear pool'. For 'to a mind that is "still" the whole universe surrenders'.[2]

How the 'power' works is a question upon which the Taoists writers throw very little light. According to one explanation[3] it is a question of equilibrium. The perfect poise that Quietism gives to the mind can for example communicate itself to the hand, and so to whatever the hand holds. The case is cited of a philosopher who possessed this 'poise' to such a degree that he could land huge fish from a deep pool with a line consisting of a single filament of raw silk. A line snaps at the point where most strain is put upon it. But if, owing to the perfect equilibrium of the fisherman's hand, no such point exists, the slenderest thread can bear the greatest imaginable weight without breaking. The Taoists indeed saw in many arts and crafts the utilization of a power akin to if not identical with that of Tao. The wheelwright, the carpenter, the butcher, the bowman, the swimmer, achieve their skill not by accumulating facts concerning their art, nor by the energetic use either of muscles or outward senses;

---

[1] VI. i. ii.   [2] *Chuang Tzŭ* XIII. i.
[3] *Lieh Tzŭ* V. 8. My interpretation of the passage differs from that of Wieger and Maspero.

but through utilizing the fundamental kinship which, underneath apparent distinctions and diversities, unites their own Primal Stuff to the Primal Stuff of the medium in which they work. Like Tao itself every 'art' is in the last resort incommunicable. Some forms of mysticism have laid stress on an oral tradition, not communicable in books; we are indeed often told that the whole Wisdom of the East is enshrined in such a tradition. Taoism went much further. Not only are books the mere discarded husk or shell of wisdom, but words themselves, expressing as they do only such things as belong to the normal state of consciousness, are irrevelant to the deeper experience of Tao, the 'wordless doctrine'. If then the Taoist speaks and still more if he writes, he does so merely to arouse interest in his doctrines, and not in any hope of communicating what another cannot be made to feel any more than you can feel the pain in my finger.

The Language Crisis

During the fourth century B.C. it began to occur to the Chinese that words move in a world of their own, a region connected only in the most casual and precarious way with the world of reality. Sometimes the mere presence of a particular word in a sentence is sufficient to label that sentence as connected solely with the region of words and not at all with the world of actualities. Such a word is 'infinite', whether applied to the infinitely small or the infinitely great. Take a stick a foot long.[1] Halve it. To-morrow halve that half, and so on day after day. Ten thousand generations hence there will still, theoretically

[1] *Chuang Tzŭ* XXXIII. 7. For the question of Hellenistic influence see Appendix II.

speaking, be something left to halve. But in reality we are obliged to stop short much sooner than this, even though we may suppose that with better eyes and a sharper knife we could still go on. In the same way it can be shown that any sentence containing the word 'infinite' belongs to the world of language, not to that of facts. Not that these two domains are totally disconnected. They share a considerable amount of common ground. Many words can be regarded as labels of particular objects, and in such cases it might seem as though there were a close correspondence between the two worlds. Unfortunately this correspondence ceases when several labels are combined; as is indeed true of actual labels in real life. For one can pile eight labels marked 'elephant' one on top of another;[1] but one cannot pile eight elephants on top of another. One can in fact (which is often very convenient) say things that sound all right, but mean nothing at all.

Now there were particular reasons, connected with the history and character not only of the Chinese language, but also of the script, which made this rift between language and actuality not merely a subject of detached philosophic enquiry, as has been the case elsewhere, not merely an easily tolerated inconvenience (as we are apt to regard it) but a burning question of the day. Chinese vocabulary was built up from a comparatively small number of original roots by a long series of meaning-extensions. The same process can of course be seen at work in all languages. But whereas this was in Chinese during its formative period the only process by which vocabulary was enriched,[2] in most other civilized languages another

[1] This image of the elephants is mine and is not used by the Chinese.

[2] No doubt isolated foreign words may have found their way into

process was going on at the same time. For example in Japan no doubt a certain amount of meaning-extension applied to native roots has been going on since the 6th century A.D. But by far the greater number of additions to Japanese vocabulary has been made by borrowing Chinese words; and it may be said in a general way that if the Japanese wanted a new word they turned at once to Chinese, just as we to-day turn to Latin or Greek. The absence of similar borrowing and the free use of meaning-extension in ancient China had the result that the same word meant a great many different things. Thus *hsiang* meant elephant,[1] and hence ivory. Hence carved ivory tablets representing omen-objects,[2] hence anything that 'stood for' or represented something else; an image or symbol. Finally, though not, I think till well after the Christian era, the word came to mean 'like', 'as', 're-sembling', as it does in current Chinese to-day. Or to take another example, the word *ssŭ*, which now means a temple, comes from a root the basic meaning of which is 'to take in hand'. Hence (1) to hold on to in order to control. (2) to hold on to in order to support oneself. (3) a place where things are 'taken in hand', where business is handled, a courtroom. Finally, official premises assigned to foreigners for worship, and hence a Buddhist temple.[3] The words in such a series are all variations of the same root. But they were in many cases distinguished by slight

early Chinese. But no considerable influx took place till the populariz-ation of Buddhism in the early centuries of the Christian era.

[1] The elephant did not become extinct in China till about the 5th century B.C. It is said still to exist in parts of Yünnan.

[2] A species of domino was used in divination till quite late times.

[3] Compare the word 'basilikon'. It is not certain that all the examples given are semantic developments. Possibly *hsiang* (elephant) and *hsiang* (symbol) are separate words.

differences of sound, which in process of time often developed into considerable divergencies. If Chinese had not been a written language, it would in many cases have soon been forgotten that the words in such series of meaning-extensions had any connection with one another at all. But for the fact that they are still written with the same character it would not occur to anyone, for example, that *yao* 'music' and *lo* 'to rejoice' are the same word. In point of fact they both go back to an original root 'lak'.[1]

To obviate the inconvenience caused by the fact that the same character stood for perhaps a dozen different developments of meaning, scribes took to writing what are called 'determinatives'[2] alongside of the characters. Thus when the 'hold on to' root meant 'hold in order to control' they wrote the character 'hand' at the side of it, to make sure there should be no mistake. But when it meant 'hold on to for support' and hence 'rely upon', 'have confidence in', they added the character 'heart'. Egyptian scribes, to name only one parallel, did just the same thing. But until the 3rd century B.C. this helpful practice was carried out very irregularly and inadequately. Thus in writing, different meanings of the same character were occasionally distinguished, but more often no such distinction was made; and in speech, some meaning-extensions were marked by differences of intonation or small variations in sound, but a great many were absolutely identical in pronunciation and if divorced from their context could equally well mean any of half a dozen different things.

In all languages it is the smallest and most innocent-

[1] Or 'glak', according to the current view. But I am inclined to regard the 'g' as a prefix and not part of the root. [2] Or radicals.

looking words which have given rise to the most trouble. A large number of the tangles in which European thinkers have involved themselves have been due to the fact that the verb 'to be' means a great many different things. The fact that Chinese lacks anything exactly corresponding to the verb 'to be' might at first sight seem to put Chinese logicians at an initial advantage. But this is far from being the case. Chinese assertions take the form 'commence begin indeed', i.e. 'To commence is to begin'. And this pattern of words, attended upon by the harmless-looking particle *yeh*, 'indeed', has caused by its reticence far more trouble than any Western copulative by its assertiveness. Some of the things that this simple pattern can express are as follows: (1) Identity, as in the example given above; (2) that A is a member of a larger class, B. For example 'Boat wooden-thing indeed', i.e. 'boats are made of wood'; (3) that A has a quality B. For example 'Tail long indeed', i.e. 'its tail is long'.[1] If words have a fixed connection with realities, the Chinese argued, *yeh* ('indeed') ought always to mean the same thing. If for example it implies identity, one ought to be able to travel hundred of leagues on any 'wooden-thing'; but in point of fact one can only travel on a boat.

The absence of a plural led to similar difficulties. 'One horse is a horse' was expressed by 'One horse, horse indeed'. 'Two horses are horses' (i.e. belong to the category 'horse') was expressed by 'Two horse, horse indeed'. It appears then that in the world of language one horse is

[1] This is in reality only a special case of (2); for the category of 'long things' is a large class, embracing such tails as happen to be long. But the Chinese regarded 'qualities' in rather a different light, looking upon them as 'something added to' the thing in question.

identical with two horses; we know that in the world of
fact this is not so. But not only did Chinese nouns lack
number; Chinese verbs lacked tense. This creates another
barrier between language and reality. If we say 'Yao sage
indeed' this can only refer to the past; for Yao lived
thousands of years ago. Consequently when we say
'Orphan, child minus-parent indeed' (i.e. an orphan is a
child without parents), it ought to mean that an orphan
is a child that never had any parents, for the same formula
of words has been shown to refer, in the case of Yao, to
the past, not to the present.

The people who discussed those difficulties—in Europe
they have generally been called Sophists, but the Chinese
called them 'discriminators' (*pien*)—did so not in order to
prove, for example, that orphans never had parents, but to
show how dangerous is the gulf that separates language
from reality. The problem was not an abstract one; indeed, if it had been, the Chinese would not have been
interested in it. For all Chinese philosophy is essentially
the study of how men can best be helped to live together
in harmony and good order.[1] It is only through language
(*ming*), through 'orders' (*ming*, written differently but
etymologically the same word) that this help can be given.
Nothing is more harmful to a state than that different
realities should share a common name; nothing more
dangerous than that theories and doctrines which belong
only to the world of language should be mistaken for
truths concerning the world of fact. In the domain of
language, as we have seen, the same formula expresses a

[1] 'Order (in a State) is the supreme good; disorder the supreme
evil.' *Kuan Tzŭ*, 47, end.

whole series of relationships. It may mean practical identity ('To commence is to begin'); it may merely mean that
two things share certain qualities, while remaining quite
different in other respects. In language things are either
the same ('Robber man indeed') or different ('Robber
not-man indeed'). In the world of fact there are innumerable degrees of sameness and difference. A robber is the
same as a man, in that he ought not to be indiscriminately
slain; he is different from a man, in that he carries off one's
property, whereas men in general do not. Some people,
not understanding how great a gulf lies between the
world of words and the world of fact, claim that since a
robber 'is different from a man' he may be indiscriminately slaughtered.[1]

We are very scantily informed as to the history of the
'language-reforming' movement in China. My hypothesis
is that the *pien chê* ('discriminators') were the people who
discovered and to some extent analysed the discrepancy
between language and reality. No doubt there were some
among them who exploited this discovery in a merely
frivolous way, startling and bewildering their audiences
by the paradoxes that ensue if one accepts the statements
of the language-world as true of our world, or *vice versa*.
But as regards the existence of such a class of 'sophists' we
are dependent on hearsay, and it is quite certain that the

[1] See *Mo Tzŭ*, P'ien 44. *Hsün Tzŭ*, P'ien 22. Hu Shih's *Wên Ts'un* II.
35 seq. The school of Mo Tzŭ took up the language question in the
third century very much in the same way that some Churchmen to-day
have taken up psycho-analysis, in order to arm themselves against
modernist attack. What survives of these Mohist language-studies is a
glossary of terms used by the 'discriminators'; a commentary on that
glossary, and a memoria technica of replies to awkward questions.

average man must have regarded the whole business about 'a white horse being or not being a horse' and attributes 'not being mutually exclusive' as mere quibbling; so that in popular imagination even the most impeccably serious logicians must in any case have figured as charlatans.

Another serious difficulty was caused by the particular type of meaning-extension which is exemplified in the word *i*, 'morality'. No one was inconvenienced by the fact that *hou*, which originally meant 'a target for arrows' had come also to mean 'a chieftain, a feudal lord'; for this was merely a transition from one concrete meaning to another, and the context always made it clear which meaning was intended. With the 'moral' words, the case was different. *I* for example meant something entirely 'external' and objective, it had been applied to acts concordant with the circumstances, to behaviour such as tradition taught people to demand and expect. But now the Confucians insisted that it was something existing inside one, a sort of extra 'sense', built up and nourished by particular sorts of behaviour. The school of Mo Tzŭ also attached the greatest importance to *i*.[1] It was 'most precious of all the ten thousand things'. But whereas with them it manifested itself in loving every one equally, to the Confucians nothing was more damaging to *i* than to love anyone else as much as one loved one's parents. This claim on the part of the moralists to the possession of a special 'sense' was as irritating to the general public as is the claim of modern æsthetes to a special æsthetic sense. Both Confucians and Mohists demanded that the

[1] *Mo Tzŭ*, P'ien 47, beginning.

whole administration of government should be put in the hands of the 'morally superior' (*hsien*); but when it came to deciding who these 'morally superior' were, they could not agree. In the minds of practical people a suspicion arose that *i*, like the conception 'infinite' and so many other high-sounding creations of the thinker as opposed to the man of action, belonged solely to the world of language and had no counterpart at all in actual life.

The theoretical object of the 'Ming Chia' (Language Students) was to amend language so that 'every different reality should be expressed by a different word', and this having been achieved no one should in future be allowed 'to split up existing meanings and make them into new words'.[1] Such an aim was of course, as regards ordinary parlance, quite impossible to realize. It had its effect, however, upon writing; for it was at this time (in the 4th and 3rd centuries) that the use of 'determinatives' to distinguish between different meaning-extensions of the same word began to come into much more general use.

Curiously enough the rather fruitless controversy about the improvement of language ended by escaping on to more practical ground through a loophole that admirably illustrated how urgent the need for improvement was. The word for realities as opposed to names ('language') is *hsing*, which originally meant 'shape'; hence to alter in shape, to mutilate, and so 'to punish'; for in early China punishment consisted in cutting off the nose, the ears, the feet, etc. Nowadays these two senses ('shape' and 'punishment') are distinguished in writing by the use of different determinatives. But in early China this was not

[1] *Hsün Tzŭ*, P'ien 22.

the case. Thus it came about that the controversy concerning 'words and realities' wandered off unperceived on to fresh ground, becoming in the end merely a discussion about the fitting of words (i.e. definition of crimes) to 'shapings' (i.e. their appropriate punishments).

The Realists[1]

China throughout the period that I have been discussing consisted of a number of small kingdoms, and the only state of affairs known to the Chinese by actual experience or in the records of history[2] (as opposed to mythology) was one of continual assaults and counterassaults, raids and reprisals. Efforts to mitigate this state of continual discord and violence were not wanting. Treaties, pacts, truces, alliances followed fast upon one another. But the intentions of those who made them were not peaceable; and when, as inevitably happened, the conflict was renewed, it was further exacerbated by heated recriminations over the purely technical question as to which side had first violated the pact. At the turn of the fourth and third centuries the States of Chao and Ch'in entered into the following agreement: 'From this time henceforward in whatever Ch'in desires to do she is to be assisted by Chao; and in whatever Chao desires to do she is to be assisted by Ch'in.' Soon afterwards Ch'in attacked the kingdom of Wei, and Chao made ready to go to Wei's assistance. The king of Ch'in protested that this

[1] I use this term in its everyday not its philosophical sense. Their name in Chinese is *Fa Chia*, 'Legalists', but I feel the need of a wider term.

[2] For pre-history, see Appendix V.

was an infringement of the pact. But prompted by the pacifist logician Kung-sun Lung the king of Chao replied: 'According to the pact each side guarantees to help the other in whatever either desires to do. I now desire to save the State of Wei, and if you do not help me to do so, I shall charge you with infringement of the pact.'[1]

A belief however existed that China had not always been in this unhappy condition of internecine strife and disorder. Long ago the great Ancestors had exercised undisputed sway over 'everything under heaven'; and if modern rulers had not succeeded in doing more than establishing precarious hegemonies, into which the smaller and more defenceless States were absorbed, this was only because these rulers lacked the universal and all-embracing 'power' (*tê*) that can draw to itself 'everything under heaven'. Gradually the word *Ti* ('Ancestor') took on a new sense—that of Universal Ruler. The *Ti* was awaited as a kind of Messiah, and round the belief in his coming centred, in a sense, the whole of Chinese thought. For every school (Confucians, Mohists, followers of Yang Chu, Taoists) believed that it had rediscovered the *tao*, the principle by which the ancient *Ti* had ruled over the whole 'world'. To the Chinese of this period the word One (unity, singleness, etc.) had an intensely emotional connotation, reflected equally in political theory and in Taoist metaphysics. And indeed the longing, or more accurately the psychological need for a fixed standard of belief was profounder, more urgent and more insistent than the longing for governmental unity. In the long run man cannot exist without an orthodoxy, without a fixed

[1] *Lü Shih Ch'un Ch'iu*, P'ien 105.

pattern of fundamental belief. It is hard for us to-day who live in societies, like those of France or England, which despite a surface of moral anarchy, are in fact rooted upon Christian ethics, to imagine such a state of chaos as existed in China in the fourth and third centuries. The old auguristic-sacrificial outlook had, at any rate among the ruling classes, completely lost its hold, and in its place had sprung up a series of doctrines each differing from the other on questions that profoundly affected the interpretation of man's life and destiny. This is all the harder for us to realize because we are accustomed to view this period through the spectacles of a later, Confucian orthodoxy which knew little or nothing of the struggles by which it had itself been achieved. Nor even within the main schools of thought was there any semblance of an interior orthodoxy. Confucianism, for example, towards the middle of the 3rd century, was divided into eight schools each claiming to be the sole repository of the Master's teaching.[1] Every Court in China was infested by 'journeying philosophers', each in turn pressing upon a bewildered ruler the claims of Activism, of Quietism, of morality, of non-morality, of force, of non-resistance, of individualism, of State supremacy. In one thing only were they united; each claimed to possess the secret 'art of ruling' whereby the Ancestors had grown mighty in the past.

But in the minds of those who actually handled practical affairs a suspicion arose that the past could not be re-created. Obvious cultural changes such as the introduction of iron[2] and the use of cavalry, with all the changes of

[1] *Han Fei Tzŭ*, P'ien 50.
[2] There are references to iron in the *Yü kung* and *Tso Chuan*. But the

costume and equipment which this latter innovation involved, suggested that the Ancestors lived in a very
different world. The question whether they achieved
their supremacy by force, by 'morality', by *yoga*, by using
only 'one word for one fact' or by correct performance of
rites and ceremonies was not one which necessarily had
any bearing on this very different, modern world. There
arose a school of Realists, who saw no need for abstract
principles such as morality and benevolence, nor for the
consecration of particular emotions such as pity or love.
The principles that should guide life do not need to be
deduced from theories about the Five Elements, the
Seasons, the Planets, the relation of Nine Times Nine to
Eight Times Eight.[1] The only fundamental and relevant
principles are inherent in the nature of life itself. Man
needs food, clothing and shelter. To prate to him of
benevolence, morality, universal love and so on, when he
lacks these essential things is like 'reciting the Book of
Odes to a fish out of water'. To produce food and clothing he must have fields for his rice or corn, orchards for
his mulberry-trees.[2] There must be a roof over his head.
To preserve these essential things for the community is
the fundamental duty of the State (*kuo*) or, put in other
words, of the ruler (*chu*) as symbol of the State, and all

Yü kung is now generally thought to date from the beginning of the 4th
century, and there is another version of the *Tso Chuan* story, in which
the word 'iron' does not occur. Iron was at first used mainly for agricultural implements, and not till the Han dynasty(?) for weapons of
war.

[1] For the place of numerical conceptions in Chinese thought, see
Granet's recent work, *La Pensée Chinoise*.
[2] Upon the leaves of which silkworms were fed.

other State activities are subordinate to this. Territory, then—fields, orchards and pastures—is the very life of the people, and to keep territory intact force is necessary. Other methods have been tried, but where are the States that tried them? Their national altars have been cast down, their citizens enslaved or slaughtered, their territories divided among the powerful. A philosopher from the country of Chêng asked for an audience with the king of Chao. Hoping for entertaining subtleties, the king sent for him. 'What are you going to talk to me about?' he asked. The philosopher said he proposed to talk about war. 'But I am not at all fond of war,' the king protested. The philosopher rubbed his hands, gazed at the ceiling and laughed. 'I never supposed you were,' he said, 'for of all hairy-ape games war is the vilest. . . . But suppose a strong and covetous State had concentrated its armies on your frontiers and were demanding land. Much use would it be to discourse to them upon abstract principles (*li*) or morality (*i*). In a word, so long as your Majesty does not arm, the neighbouring kingdoms can do with you as they will.' The king of Chao said: 'Tell me how to arm.'[1]

The period was one of profound disillusionment. Mencius in the second half of the 4th century had preached with exaltation and fervour the fundamental goodness of man's nature. Nowhere had the new doctrine of 'morality and kindness' been so generally accepted as in the small State of Lu, the home of Confucianism. Yet in 249 Lu was invaded and destroyed. Small wonder if Hsün Tzŭ, writing at about the time of the fall of Lu, some thirty years or more after the death of Mencius,

1 *Chan Kuo Ts'ê*, VI. 49.

reverses his predecessor's doctrine. Man's nature, says
Hsün Tzŭ, is bad. He is born greedy, jealous, lustful.
Goodness is a thing that must be imposed upon him from
without, as wood is rendered serviceable by straightening
its 'obliquities' in the press. This is the view of a Confucian. The Realists went much further. Honest people
may exist. One might even find twenty or thirty of them
in a State. But of what use is a score when one is looking
for hundreds?[1] The Confucians and Mohists had insisted
that the task of government must be entrusted to *hsien*
'morally superior' people. Unfortunately the attributes of
moral superiority are so easy to counterfeit that from the
moment when it is known that *hsien* are to be promoted,
the country teems with pseudo-benevolence and pseudo-
morality.[2] The Realists were also very distrustful of what
one may call short-term emotions. Pity for individuals
too often entails cruelty towards the community at large.
They were fond of using the simile of hair-washing.[3] He
who washes his head inevitably loses a certain number of
hairs. But if for that reason one refrained from ever wash-
ing the head, there would soon be no hairs left at all. 'A
polity that does not involve hardship, national achievements (*kung*) that do not entail suffering have never yet
existed under heaven.' Life in its essence is stern and
hard:

> No lake so still but that it has its wave;
> No circle so perfect but that it has its blur.
> I would change things for you if I could;
> As I can't, you must take them as they are.[4]

[1] *Han Fei Tzŭ*, 49.   [2] *Han Fei Tzŭ*, 7.
[3] *Ibid.*, 46; repeated in 47.   [4] *Ibid.*, 47.

73

So ran an old rhyming proverb. We must take the facts of life and human nature as we find them. 'Ordinary people (*min*) are lazy; it is natural to them to shirk hard work and to delight in idleness.'[1] If in times of scarcity we give grain doles to the poor we are merely taxing those whose providence and industry have enabled them to save, in order to supply the wants of those whose own idleness and improvidence has reduced them to penury.[2] The result of such mistaken benevolence can only be general idleness, followed by general indigence and misery. The common people are incapable of looking ahead. They do not wish to be enslaved by foreigners, they do not wish to have their homes burned, but they would not if left to themselves take any long-sighted measure to prevent these disasters. 'They want security, but hate the means that produce security.' The State therefore is all the time demanding from the people things that are hard and irksome. Sophists, Confucians, Mohists, Hedonists, half a dozen other sects and persuasions, are only too ready to take advantage of this fact, and delude the people into thinking that there is a way of safety which is not 'hard'. But the Realist knows that all these doctrines are founded on illusions, on the idea that in this world of blurs and smears a perfect circle can yet be drawn. There can be no compromise with these doctrines. 'Ice and embers cannot lie in the same bowl.' 'If the horses are pulling different ways the coach will not advance.' There must be no private doctrines (*ssŭ hsüeh*); no religion indeed save that of the Realists which alone is founded on facts, not on abstractions or what is almost as

[1] *Han Fei Tzŭ*, 54.   [2] *Ibid.*, 50.

bad, on the experience of exceptional people. The philosopher Lao Tan said that 'he who is content with what he
has got can never be despoiled, he who knows when to
stop can never be destroyed'. On the basis of this some
politicians pretend that the whole object of government
is to give the people as much of everything as they can
desire; whereupon they will instantly become orderly and
contented. This might be true if the common people
were all philosophers. The only maxim true of the world
as it exists is that the more people have, the more they
want.[1] The Confucians are compared by Han Fei Tzŭ[2]
to the quack magicians who pretend that by their prayers
and incantations they can make their customers live 'a
thousand autumns, ten thousand years'; yet for all their
gabblĭngs and antics no one has ever yet been known to
obtain the slightest benefit of any kind by patronizing
them. So the Confucians pretend that by studying the
records of remote antiquity and the achievements of long-
dead kings they have discovered a secret that will enable
the modern ruler to confound his enemies. 'But the enlightened ruler pays attention only to facts and ideas that
are of practical use at the moment. He does not concern
himself with benevolence and morality; or listen to the
empty discourses of learned people.' In the remote past
the population was small and there was plenty and to
spare for everybody. It was easy enough then and in no
wise meritorious to exercise the virtues of 'sharing' and
'yielding' that the Confucians attributed to the ancient
sages. To-day everything is changed. We live in troub-
lous times and it is no more possible to rule a great modern

[1] *Han Fei Tzŭ*, 46.   [2] *Ibid.*, 50.

kingdom as though it were a village in which everyone was related to everyone else, than it is possible for a wheelbarrow to keep pace with a chariot. The wise ruler has no use for 'wheelbarrow' government.[1] Needless to say, the whole of the sacrificial-auguristic side of public life must be ruthlessly discarded. 'That a State should keep times and days, serve ghosts and spirits, trust in divination by the tortoise or by the yarrow-stalks, be fond of prayers and sacrifices, is a portent of doom.'[2] This is part of the forty-seven portents of political decay, each clause ending with the word *wang* ('doom', 'destruction') that clangs like a warning bell across these powerful and impressive pages.

The school that came perhaps into most active conflict with the Realists was that of Mo Tzŭ, whose doctrine of universal love demanded that one should 'feel towards all people under heaven exactly as one feels towards one's own people, regard other States exactly as one regards one's own State'. It becomes necessary at this point to digress a little, and see what had hitherto been the Chinese attitude to war. While the old belief in the Ancestors and Heaven (the abode of the Ancestors) was in full sway, war like every other activity was hedged round by innumerable precautions and restrictions. It was safe to attack only when one had reason to believe that the enemy had forfeited the support of their Former Kings; for 'against Heaven none can war'. This view gave rise in the moralistic period to the familiar distinction between righteous and unrighteous wars, the aggressors acting in the former

[1] *Han Fei Tzŭ*, 47.
[2] *Han Fei Tzŭ*, 15.

Introduction

as agents of Heaven, and bringing a well merited chastise-
ment to those who had sinned against Heaven. This was
particularly the case with wars resulting in the establishment of a new dynasty. Each dynastic line ends with a
wicked monarch whose sins 'cry to Heaven'. At the same
time weapons, used on behalf of whatever cause, are
'unlucky implements'.[1] The metal of which they are
made has been wrested from the earth, and earth is loth
to lose her treasures. War causes the crops to fail and the
streams to dry. It was indeed hard for the governing
classes to uproot from the minds of the people this conception of war as essentially baleful and ill-omened. Yet
not to train the people for war is to abandon them to the
mercy of their enemies. The idea that weapons are
'baleful' is combatted in the *Ta Tai Li Chi*.[2] Peace and war
are permanent features in man's environment, Confucius
is represented as saying, just as rage and delight are permanent elements in his emotional constitution. This,
however, was only the view of certain Confucian schools.
During the 4th century, when the Yang Chu doctrine
that the perfect State consists of whole and 'intact' individuals was at the height of its vogue, Confucianism too
was influenced by the individualist doctrine. It was man's
first duty to keep himself intact. So far this Confucian
school was in agreement with Yang Chu. But whereas the
followers of Yang Chu perfected the individual in order
that there might be a perfect aggregation of individuals,
the Confucian perfected himself in order that his duty
towards his parents might be carried out by a perfect

[1] Quoted as a proverbial saying by *Han Fei Tzŭ*, 2, beginning.
[2] P'ien 75, 'on the use of arms'.

individual. It is for this reason that it is his duty not to risk any diminution of his physical or mental efficiency. He may neither 'climb up on to high places nor look down into deep places'.[1] He remembers at every instant that his body is a sacred trust, committed to him by his parents. No hair, no tissue of his whole frame must ever be wilfully imperilled.[2] It is doubtful however whether this doctrine obtained much currency till the Han period. The real enemies of violence were the Mohists, and the great upholder of pacifism was the Mohist Kung-sun Lung, also famous as a logician. He succeeded in partially converting to his theories King Hui of Chao, who came to the throne in 298 B.C. 'I have now been aiming at the suppression of arms for ten years,' the king said to Kung-sun Lung one day, 'but with very little success. Don't you think the truth may be that arms cannot be suppressed?' 'The doctrine of the suppression of arms', said Kung-sun Lung, 'is the outcome of universal love, felt equally towards everyone under heaven. If such love exists only in words but not in actuality this policy can certainly not be carried out.' Kung-sun Lung goes on to point out that the king's state of mind was one which could not possibly lead to the realization of the aims which he professed. He was manifestly still obsessed by the old hatred of the western kingdom of Ch'in. When two towns voluntarily placed themselves under Ch'in rule, King Hui (the philosopher reminded him) went into mourning; but on hearing that the Ch'ins had lost a castle he celebrated the occasion by a banquet.[3] But the truth is, as a Realist

[1] *Li Chi*, I.   [2] *Book of Filial Piety*, beginning.
[3] *Lü Shih Ch'un Ch'iu*, 101.

writer[1] points out, that 'the most the benevolent man can do is to be benevolent to others; he cannot cause others to be benevolent to him. The most the moral man can do is to exercise his love upon other people; he cannot make other people love one another'. The necessity for self-defence was generally admitted, and the Mo Tzŭ school gave special attention to the arts of fortification, freely admitting that to love every one equally does not necessarily entail being loved by everyone equally. But a purely defensive policy has, as Kuan Tzŭ points out, great disadvantages. In actual practice the status of soldiering, in countries that adopt such a policy, is a low one, pay is inadequate, interest in the military arts is at a low ebb. Sooner or later the integrity of the 'defensive' State is threatened from abroad, and the only result of this 'defensive' policy is that the aggressors operate with a trained army, we with a hastily summoned levy; they are led by skilled generals, we by mere incompetents;[2] with the inevitable result. Accordingly even the State that does not contemplate aggression must foster an aggressive state of mind in the people. Even more dangerous to the State than the upholders of the purely defensive policy are those whom 'the world honours with the name of *kuei-shêng* ("esteemers of the individual life")', but who are in reality 'mere runaways, afraid for their skins'.[3] The tendency of peasant populations to shoulder their ploughs and hearth-stones and flee before an invader was one which sorely troubled early Chinese rulers. The nomadic period was indeed not so far away, and stories really belonging to

[1] *Shang Tzŭ*, 18.   [2] *Kuan Tzŭ*, 65, beginning.
[3] *Han Fei Tzŭ*, 46, beginning.

such a period could be quoted in defence of non-resistance. Had not old father Tan, a Chou Ancestor, when his territory was threatened by another tribe, successively offered them skins, silk, horses, dogs, pearls, jade, in the hopes of bribing them off; and at last finding it was land and land alone that his enemies desired, had he not quietly surrendered his territory and trekked with his tribesmen all the way from Pin to the foot of Mount Ch'i?[1] To attach the people to their homes and prevent them from trekking off, from 'evading difficulties', as such emigrations were called, at the first hint of trouble, was no easy matter.

But to return to the doctrine of the Realists. The first essential, as we have seen, was that the State should maintain its frontiers intact. The second was that the people should have food and clothing. Soldiering must be the profession that holds the highest status in the whole corporate life; and next to it must come agriculture. Admittedly the life of the peasant is much less agreeable than that of the scholar, the roaming politician, the manufacturer of luxuries and toys. For this very reason the State must do everything in its power to stem the inevitable drift from agriculture, on which the existence of the country depends, into unessential occupations. Above all, the rising influence of the merchant must be checked,[2] for the whole power of the State lies in its power to punish or reward, and the existence of a class which 'rewards itself', and consequently has no incentive to seek public reward,

[1] The story is told in *Mencius, Chuang Tzŭ, Huai-nan Tzŭ* and elsewhere. It is still popular, being cited, for example, in a recent propaganda pamphlet of the Manchukuo government.

[2] *Han Fei Tzŭ*, 49, end.

is a menace to society. The number, then, of those who enrich themselves whether by commerce or by any form of unessential craft, is to be limited to the barest minimum, and their social position is to be lowest in the State.

A vast system of punishments and rewards is indeed to take the place of any appeal to public feeling, decency or morality. For such virtues function even at best in a sporadic and irregular way and in the majority of men maintain an existence shadowy indeed when contrasted with the two active and prominent motives of mankind— 'love of profit and love of fame'. A few exceptional people can draw a perfect circle without using a compass, estimate the weight of grain without using scales; but if the making of wheels and the selling of grain depended on the use of such people, the markets would languish and waggoning soon be at a standstill. 'Morality' as apart from 'legality' is merely an unnecessary factor, disintegrating because of its uncertain and irregular operation, inconsistent with the great Realist principle of unity, in that it introduces and sanctions a sort of private, secondary Law.

Codification is, I suppose, always connected with spread of empire. In a small, homogeneous community law is merely 'what is customary'. But if other communities with other customs are conquered and absorbed it becomes necessary to decide which alien customs can be tolerated and which are inimical to the new, larger society. For it is not in practice ever possible completely to eradicate all usages save those of the conquering tribe. It is easy to see that the 'codification' movement in China was part of a general tendency towards unification of manners in the widest sense. It is reflected in the activity of the 'ritualist'

The Way and its Power

school of Confucianism which, faced with a multiplicity of conflicting usages and traditions, attempted to construct, at any rate for the *chün-tzŭ*, the upper classes, a uniform code of conduct which should embrace not only every branch of public activity, but also personal relationships and domestic life. The earliest penal code preserved is that attributed to King Mu of the Chou dynasty.[1] The object of this very confused document seems to be the justification of fines as a substitute for corporal mutilation. Such a change may be regarded on the one hand as a cultural advance, similar to the substitution of clay figures for human sacrificial victims. It certainly also represents a victory for the propertied classes, who alone were able to take advantage of the innovation and so preserve their ears and noses intact. At the same time it opened up for the State an important new source of revenue. The code of King Mu deals with punishments only. But in all later documents we find a mating of punishments and rewards, due I think to the growing influence of the Yin-yang (Dualist) School,[2] deterrents and encouragements forming as it were the 'light' and 'shade' of government. In the doctrine of the Realists this appeal to hope and fear is the only *ch'ang-tao*, the only fixed principle. Its application depends solely on the circumstances of the moment, on the nature of the tasks that the State needs to perform, on the condition of the subjects who are to perform these tasks. The type of rather crude propaganda that was used

[1] 'Book of History': *Lü Ching*. Mu probably reigned in the 9th century B.C. The document in question, however, is not history, but propaganda in justification of a social change, welded on to a legend about the wickedness and ultimate destruction of a first race of men.

[2] See below, p. 110.

to justify this doctrine is well instanced by the following story, in which Confucius is made to figure as a Legalist: The men of Lu had set fire to some bushlands to the north of their capital in order to clear the ground and make it fit for agriculture. A strong north wind sprang up, the fire spread and the capital was threatened. The duke of Lu was so much perturbed that he collected the inhabitants of the city and led them in person to the scene of the fire. But the people were soon busy chasing the game that the fire had startled, and the duke presently found himself entirely deserted. In this predicament he sent for Confucius. The sage said: 'To chase animals is pleasant; to put out a fire is hard work. So long as the chasing of animals involves no penalty and the putting out of the fire brings no reward, the fire will continue to blaze.' With the duke's permission Confucius accordingly made it known that anyone who failed to help in putting out the fire would rank as a deserter on the battlefield and be dealt with accordingly; while those who were caught running after animals would be treated as though they had violated holy ground.

The fire was completely extinguished while the order was still being circulated.[1]

The Mystic Basis of Realism

It is not surprising that all surviving expositions,[2] despite their repudiation of abstract principles and ideals, do in fact seek a foundation in Taoist mysticism. The Realist system professed to be founded solely on human

[1] *Han Fei Tzŭ*, 30, second set of 'traditions'.
[2] Except *Shang Tzŭ*; see below, p. 85.

facts, and the facts which it chose for its basis are vital ones. But they are far indeed from constituting the whole truth about man and the functions of human society. The beliefs embodied in the old auguristic-sacrificial life and afterwards transmuted by the moralists into ethical conceptions were not, as the Realists claimed, mere illusion. Just as much as the opportunist doctrine of the realists, those older beliefs were founded on facts, on fundamental actualities of human existence. True, these facts concerning as they did the subtler parts of man's equipment, were more easily overlooked than those related to the broad necessities of his physical existence; but this did not make them any the less vital. It was the failure to enquire even in the most superficial way into the nature and function of the things they sought to discard that caused the Realists to build an edifice which, despite its coherence and solidity, never became and could never hope to become a dwelling-place for the human spirit. Long sections, in works such as *Han Fei Tzǔ* and *Kuan Tzǔ*, put forward the Realist position in a complete and uncompromising form. But as I have said, these works in very frequent passages make an attempt to reconcile this position with Taoism, which in the third century had become the dominant religion of China, at any rate in the sense that it coloured the works of all other schools.[1] The Taoist maxim 'Cling to the Unity' was divested of its metaphysical sense and turned into a political maxim—the absolute unification of everything in the State. Many of the incidental tenets of Taoism could, as it happened, be

[1] cf. the strong Taoist influence on the *Chung Yung, Hsi Tzʻǔ, Mencius, Lü Shih Chʻun Chʻiu, Han Fei Tzǔ, Kuan Tzǔ*, etc.

Introduction

accepted as they stood. Taoists and Realists concurred in their contempt for *hsien* (people of superior morality), for book-learning, for morality and benevolence, for commerce and 'unnecessary' contrivances; both schools decried ceremony and advocated return to simple ways of life.

There was one State in China where simple ways (including human sacrifice) had never been abandoned. This was the north-western kingdom of Ch'in. Confucianism and, we may suppose, moralistic ideas in general, had hardly penetrated there.[1] Legend attributed to the Lord Shang, a 4th century statesman in Ch'in, an important part in the creation of Realist doctrine, though it is by no means certain that such ideas existed in China at all until the 3rd century. We possess a book called *Shang Tzŭ*, dating from the end of the 3rd century, which purports to give an account of Lord Shang's teaching. This short work[2] entirely eliminates all mysticism and idealism. It is not, like previous works of the kind, a receipt for maintaining frontiers intact, with the vaguely suggested possibility of uniting several states into some sort of hegemony. It is an exaltation of war; a handbook for the rearing of a race of conquerors. 'At home and in the streets, at their eating and at their drinking, all the songs that the people sing shall be of war.'[3] 'The father shall send his son, the elder brother his younger brother, the wife her husband,

[1] *Hsün Tzŭ*, P'ien 16.
[2] Admirably edited and translated by J. J. L. Duyvendak (Probsthain's Oriental Series, Vol. XVII. 1928), under the title *The Book of Lord Shang*. I here give only a very cursory account of *Shang Tzŭ* and refer the reader to Duyvendak's introduction.
[3] *Shang Tzŭ*, 17.

each saying when she speeds him: "Conquer, or let me never see you again!" '

The Ch'in conquered; and in 221 B.C. the king of Ch'in, which till a generation or two ago had been a small, outlying, insignificant principality, became First Emperor of all China. It seemed as though at any rate the efficiency of Realism had been triumphantly demonstrated. But some ten years later the new dynasty was already tottering, and in 206 it disappeared. Those who founded it believed that a State based upon 'facts' and not upon sentimental 'illusions' such as compassion and morality, would necessarily be eternal. This belief, however, soon turned out to be itself another example of illusion.

The 'Tao Tê Ching'

About 240 B.C. an anonymous[1] Quietist produced a small book, in only two *p'ien*, known from the early centuries of the Christian era onwards as the *Tao Tê Ching*. It was an extremely polemical work, directed in the main against the Realists, but at the same time siding with them in their condemnation of Confucianism and of the doctrines of Yang Chu. A superficial reader, dipping into the early parts of the book, might easily have supposed that he had before him another of those treatises, so fashionable at the time, in which the ruthless doctrines of the Realists were diluted with a specious basis of Taoist mysticism. He would have found that the art of ruling consisted in 'emptying the people's minds and filling their bellies, weakening their wills[2] and strengthening their

[1] For the circumstances which led posterity to connect the work with the name of Lao Tzŭ, see below, p. 106.

[2] cf. *Shang Tzŭ*, P'ien 20.

bones', in 'treating the hundred families like straw dogs', that is to say, not allowing any private feelings of pity towards individuals, any short-range sentimentalities to stand in the way of the general will of the State. He would have found this anonymous author using with apparent approval such Realist slogans as *wu-ssŭ*, 'nothing private', that is to say, the State can tolerate no aims, no opinions, no activities that are not its own. He would have found the usual Realist condemnation of book-learning (i.e. the study of the past, which may lead to dangerous criticisms of the present), of government by *hsien* (morally superior persons), of that private and individual law which we call conscience and which the Confucians of Mencius's school called *i*. Such a reader, if we may suppose him not to have had much of an eye for subtleties or ironies, might have read on happily through more than a quarter of the work, believing himself in perfectly safe and conventional hands, till he came to the statement that 'kingdoms cannot be made strong by force of arms; for such a policy recoils on the heads of those who use it'. At this point it becomes clear that the author is not a safe or sound person at all; and such a view of him is amply confirmed by subsequent passages in which he undermines the very corner-stone of Realist domestic policy by declaring that capital punishment, mutilations, imprisonment and the like do not in point of fact act as deterrents from crime.

The Realists called themselves *fa chia*, 'Legalists', and their doctrine was based on the idea that the decadence of the State is due to its tolerating private standards of good and evil, and failing clearly to 'label', to give names (*ming*) to the things that are good and evil from the public point of view. This leads to a discrepancy between 'names' and 'facts' (i.e. realities as conceived of by the State), creates in the network of Law innumerable loopholes, of which interests hostile to the public good will not scruple to avail themselves.

The author of the *Tao Tê Ching* combats, in the first place, the idea that there is such a thing as 'public good'. Society is a complicated structure, consisting of myriads of individuals, 'some blowing hot, some blowing cold, some loading, some setting down'. The ambition of the State to 'join the tallies', to absorb all these conflicting interests in one central purpose, is futile. The most it can do is to benefit some individuals at the expense of others. Equally delusive is its claim to save society by attaching an unalterable name to every fact. For the Quietist knows that the vast majority of facts—all those, indeed, that he becomes aware of when the ordinary sense-channels are closed—have no names, are in their very essence Nameless. Yet it is the knowledge of these nameless facts, the existence of which is undreamt of by the Realist, that gives *tê*, the only power that can 'benefit without harming', that can dissolve the myriad contradictions and discordances of phenomenal existence. The mysticism of the *Tao Tê Ching* is, then, essentially that of earlier Taoist works, save that owing to the rise of the Realist school, the question of 'names' is not merely a metaphysical one, but has become topical and controversial.

Another controversy of the times, which finds prominence in the *Tao Tê Ching*, centred round the word *yü*, 'desire'. Yü does not merely mean sexual desire (though it includes this), but all the desires of all the senses, the desire of the eye for human beauty,[1] of the ear for music, of the mouth for pleasant tastes, and so on. Doctors held that the unrestricted gratification of desires was dangerous to health;[2] moralists, that it diminished the powers of conscience,[3] which was conceived of, as has been shown above, as a sort of *shên* or divinity, precariously housed in the human frame. That abstinence touches the hearts of heavenly spirits, that the presence or help of such spirits can only be obtained by fasting and self-denial, was a principle universally admitted in the sacrificial-auguristic stage of Chinese society. The Taoists believed that by 'desirelessness' (*wu yü*) the ruler could become possessed of a *tê* ('power') which would turn his subjects away from their unruly desires.[4] Precisely the same view is reflected, I think, in the passage of the *Analects*[5] where in response to a question about how to deal with robbers Confucius says: 'If only you yourself were desireless they would not steal even if you paid them to.' The commentators have been at pains to deprive the passage of its Taoist flavour.

Mo Tzŭ believed in universal love, the natural corollary of which was the abolition of war. We have seen Mo Tzŭ's follower Kung-sun Lung finding that, though people were willing to subscribe to these principles in theory, their real state of mind was entirely inconsistent with a policy of peace and goodwill. The obstacle, so Sung Tzŭ[6] discovered in the second half of the 4th century

[1] *Sê.*   [2] cf. *Tso Chuan*, Chao Kung, year 1 (Legge, p. 573).
[3] *Mencius*, VII. 2. 35.   [4] *Chuang Tzŭ*, XII. 1.   [5] XII. 18.
[6] See *Mencius*, VI. 2. 4, *Chuang Tzŭ*, I. 3 and XXXIII. 3, *Hsün Tzŭ*, P'ien 18 and *Han Fei Tzŭ*, P'ien 50. Sung's personal name is written in three different ways; but all point to an approximate Archaic

B.C., was the prevalent belief that the 'desires' which cause conflict and mutual distrust are deeply-rooted and numerous. On the contrary, man's desires are 'shallow and few'; to prove which Sung Tzŭ deployed, as *Hsün Tzŭ* tells us, a great wealth of argument and imagery. But the most convincing proof that 'desire' can be practically eliminated lay in the life led both by Sung himself and by his numerous disciples: 'Constantly rebuffed but never discouraged, they went round from State to State helping people to settle their differences, arguing against wanton attack and pleading for the suppression of arms, that the age in which they lived might be saved from its state of continual war.[1] To this end they interviewed princes and lectured the common people, nowhere meeting with any great success, but obstinately persisting in their task, till kings and commoners alike grew weary of listening to them. Yet undeterred they continued to force themselves on people's attention. Troublesome though they were, it must be confessed that what they did on behalf of others was unlimited; while what they asked for themselves was little indeed. They said all they needed was to have half a peck of rice in store. Often enough the master himself got little to eat and the disciples even less. But never for a moment did they forget what they had vowed to do for all people under heaven, and hungry though they were, never

Chinese *gieng* or *giweng*. The lack of uniformity is due to the fact that he 'travelled about everywhere under heaven'; consequently the name is preserved in various dialectal forms.

[1] We know from *Mencius* that Sung based his argument against war on expediency (*li*), that is to say, on the plea that war does not 'pay'. Mencius attributes Sung's failure to this fact, and urges him to base his appeal on moral grounds.

rested either by night or day. . . . They thought indeed that anyone who is not helping all people under heaven had far better be dead.'[1]

But Hsün Tzŭ in his chapter on the necessity of improving language,[2] shows that those who claim to be 'without desire' or to have 'few desires' are not expressing themselves accurately. In reality they have just as many desires as other people; but they have decided not to satisfy these desires. There does indeed exist a state in which desire is absent. But this state is death. We must not assume then either that we can abolish desires or that there would be any advantage in doing so. On the contrary, we must help people to choose wisely among their desires, selecting for gratification those which 'pay', those which do not stand in the way of too many other gratifications. It is simply, says Hsün Tzŭ, a matter of doing a sum, of 'counting the cost', of balancing profit and loss just as is done every day in the market-place.

The *Tao Tê Ching* uses the two expressions *wu-yü* 'desirelessness' and *kua-yü* 'reduction of desires' interchangeably. Absence or at any rate a relative absence of desire is accepted by the author of this book, as indeed by all Taoists, as an essential for the practice of Quietism.

The Shêng

The Taoists however did not, I think, ever envisage a whole community or society consisting of ascetics. The way of life discussed in their books is believed by them to be an old one. It was followed by the *shêng*, the sage Ancestors who ruled mute and motionless over the em-

[1] *Chuang Tzŭ*, XXXIII. 3.   [2] *Hsün Tzŭ*, XXII. Paragraph 9.

pires of the past. True, the subjects of these Sages were insensibly led in a Quietist direction; but it is never suggested that they themselves actually practised Quietism or became possessed of its mysterious 'power'. The *Tao Tê Ching* is not in intention (though anyone may treat it as such, if he so chooses) a way of life for ordinary people.[1] It is a description of how the Sage (*shêng*) through the practice of Tao acquires the power of ruling without being known to rule. In Chinese, as we have seen, tense is not usually expressed. Every sentence in the *Tao Tê Ching* refers as much to the past as to the present. 'The Sage does this or that' means that the Sages of the past did so and that anyone who wishes to possess their miraculous power must do so again. Throughout the book it is assumed (as everyone except the Realists assumed) that an ideal state of society once existed. All reform simply means a return to the remote past. A very remote past indeed; for as far back as history went—that is to say, to the 8th century B.C.—no trace could be discovered of anything save just such violence and disorder as still prevailed in the 3rd century. But behind the historic period stretched legendary epochs which, though removed from the present by whole millennia seemed, and to a great extent still seem to the Chinese much nearer than the historic past. For mythology was in a fluid state, and these legendary eras could, from generation to generation, be remoulded to suit current longings and aspirations. Thus though nothing new could be recommended that was not according to the way of the Ancestors, the

[1] In *Chuang Tzŭ*, however, Taoism is in certain passages treated as a way of life for individual adepts.

Introduction

Ancestors themselves could be reformed. Ku Chieh-kang[1] has shown the humanizing process through which the legend of the San Miao, a race of rebellious 'first men', has passed. In the first stage of the legend the Supreme Ancestor annihilates them. In the second, they are banished to a remote corner of the earth. In the final stage, they are peacefully converted by a display of *tê*, of magico-moral 'power'. And it is by *tê*, not by war, that the Sage of the *Tao Tê Ching* 'wins the adherence of all under heaven'. Such a method is indeed the only one consistent with Quietism.[2] What strikes us at first sight as inconsistent with Quietism is the idea of founding an empire at all. By the middle of the third century, however, it had been generally recognized that the peace for which everyone longed could only come through the unification of China under one strong State. It was believed that such a unification had existed in the past, and all political thought of the period centered upon schemes for the restoration of this hypothetical Empire. But often it seems as though cultural rather than political conquest were envisaged. 'A nation,' Mussolini has said,[3] 'becomes imperial when directly or indirectly it rules other nations; it need not necessarily have conquered a single yard of territory.' The actual territory of the Ancestors Yao and Shun is often said, by those who believed most fervently in the existence of the early Empire, not to have extended more than a few miles. But the whole of China was subject to their 'power'. It is as well to bear this in mind when reading the political chapters of the *Tao Tê Ching*.

[1] *Ku Shih Pien.* Introduction, p. 53.
[2] As is indeed stated in the *Tao Tê Ching*, Ch. 30.
[3] *Enciclopedia Italiana*, Vol. 14.

The Way and its Power

An important difference between this book and other Taoist works is its attitude towards war. We have seen that pacificism arose out of the 'universal love' of Mo Tzŭ, and was preached at the close of the 4th century B.C. by the logician Kung-sun Lung and the altruist Sung Tzŭ. In the whole of the great Taoist corpus which is constituted by the forty one *p'ien* of *Chuang Tzŭ* and *Lieh Tzŭ* there is no specific condemnation of war. It is assumed as self-evident that violence of any kind is contrary to the principles of Tao, which 'acts' only through its own specific *tê* or 'power'. The *Tao Tê Ching* however devotes three chapters (30, 31 and 69) to the condemnation of war, and though chapter 31 has unfortunately reached us in a corrupt state, it is quite clear what the views of the author are. In condemning war he is addressing not the Quietist, whose principles in any case forbade violent action, but the average 'worldly person'. He cannot like Mencius appeal to morality, for two reasons: in the first place, the existence of morality (as opposed to legality) was no longer generally admitted; and secondly, the Quietist system itself rejected such conceptions as morality and altruism. He might like Sung Tzŭ have attempted to meet the common man on his own ground, by proving that apart from all moral or religious considerations, war is to be condemned, like any other bad bargain, for the simple reason that it costs more than it is worth. This is one of the arguments used by the Mo Tzŭ school.[1] A small castle may often cost as much as 10,000 lives. Multiply 'victories' indefinitely and you will have a vast territory, but no soldiers left to defend it. The same sort of argument,

[1] *Mo Tzŭ*, P'ien 18.

based on 'profit and loss', was apparently used by Sung Tzŭ. Such appeals to the mercantile spirit meet with a response only from those who are already opposed to war. Among primitive peoples the object of war is to renew the waning vigour of the tribe,[1] and wherever the warring instinct survives it is grounded not in a belief that war pays in the material sense, but in the belief that (as a modern Fascist writer has said) 'it sets once more the stamp of nobility upon a people'. Mo Tzŭ, however,- makes an alternative appeal to the belief of the masses. 'Whoever slays men', he says,[2] 'is destroying those upon whom Spirits depend for their sustenance, and is thus at the same time annihilating Former Kings.' The warrior, then, as has already been pointed out, is at grips not only with his own kind, but with unseen Powers whose existence, no less than that of their descendants, is at stake. It may be that the Ancestors in Heaven are disgusted with their descendants and are ready to come over to our side; indeed 'Heaven's hatreds are unaccountable'. But in general war is 'unlucky', that is to say, it is bound to give offence somewhere in the Halls of Heaven, and the result will be pest, famine, earthquakes, storms, eclipses. It is on this line of argument, directly based on *Mo Tzŭ*, that the *Tao Tê Ching* condemns offensive war, while admitting (like Mo Tzŭ and unlike the 'life-esteemers' of the Yang Chu school) the right of the community to defend itself against attack.

In chapter 31, which deals with war, a commentary[3] has

[1] By absorbing, through various rites ranging from cannibalism to drinking out of the enemy's skull, etc., the vigour and valour of another tribe.   [2] *Ibid.*, P'ien 19.   [3] Possibly that of Wang Pi (3rd century A.D.), see below, pp. 129 and 182.

become incorporated in the text. Numerous efforts have been made to restore the chapter to its original state. Not one of these yields anything that at all resembles the usual style of the *Tao Tê Ching*, with its paradoxical twisting-round of other people's maxims, its epigrammatic and pungent quality. I am inclined to think that the author has here inserted with very little adaptation a passage from some lost pacifist work of the Mo Tzŭ school.

The Literary Methods of the Book

All argument consists in proceeding from the known to the unknown, in persuading people that the new thing you want them to think is not essentially different from or at any rate is not inconsistent with the old things they think already. This is the method of science, just as much as it is the method of rhetoric and poetry. But, as between science and forms of appeal such as poetry, there is a great difference in the nature of the link that joins the new to the old. Science shows that the new follows from the old according to the same principles that built up the old. 'If you don't accept what I now ask you to believe,' the scientist says, 'you have no right to go on believing what you believe already.' The link used by science is a logical one. Poetry and rhetoric are also concerned with bridging the gap between the new and the old; but they do not need to build a formal bridge. What they fling across the intervening space is a mere filament such as no sober foot would dare to tread. But it is not with the sober that poetry and eloquence have to deal. Their *tê*, their essential power, consists in so intoxicating us that, endowed with the recklessness of drunken men, we dance across the chasm, hardly aware how we reached the other side. The appeal of the *Tao Tê Ching* is entirely of this second kind. 'What others have taught', says the author, 'I too will teach.' We are not, he promises, to be tempted across any chasm. Our feet are firmly planted on the safe, familiar shore. Yet long before we have closed the book we find to our astonishment that the chasm is behind us. Magically, without bridge or ferry, we have been transported to the other shore.

Proverbs of the people and of the patricians (*chün-tzŭ*), maxims of the strategist and realist, of the individualist (Yang Chu school); above all, sayings of the older Taoists which though they had very little apparent influence on conduct were at that period accepted as 'spiritual' truths, much as the Sermon on the Mount is accepted to-day— all these conflicting elements the author of the *Tao Tê Ching* reproduces or adapts, subtly weaving them together into a pattern perfectly harmonious and consistent, yet capable of embracing and absorbing the most refractory elements. The method here carried to an extreme point was not in itself new or exceptional. A great part of ancient thought, whether Christian, Buddhist or Mohammedan takes the form of giving fresh contents and hence new meanings to accepted maxims. Often these maxims were embodied in texts the letter of which was immune from criticism. But such texts were for a variety of reasons[1] fragmentary and ambiguous. They left ample

[1] Absence of 'determinatives' made early Chinese writing a very imperfect form of notation. Absence of vowels had the same effect in Semitic texts. Religious texts tend in general to be in obsolete or foreign languages.

room for manipulation, could be interpreted literally or figuratively, could in fact within certain limits be made to mean whatever the interpreter desired. Never has such manipulation been handled more ingeniously than by the Confucian school in China, particularly from the 1st century B.C. onwards when Confucianism had become a national orthodoxy. But in the 3rd century no such orthodoxy existed and the *Tao Tê Ching*, not being addressed exclusively to Confucians, to Mohists, to Taoists or to any one of the Twelve Schools, but comprehensively to the public at large, applies the method of 'reinterpretation' not only to the maxims of each philosophic school in turn, but also to the traditional code of thought and conduct embodied in proverbs whether plebeian or patrician.

The whole of 3rd century thought is shaken and shuffled like a kaleidoscope. Black is no longer black, nor white, white. One by one each cherished stand-by, each pivot of thought collapses, sheds its trappings and accessories, returns with no apparent intervention on the author's part to the 'state of the Uncarved Block'. The literary method of the book is indeed a triumphant exhibition of *tê*, of the 'power' that masters all complicated, all difficult and recalcitrant things by reducing them to their alternative state of unity and simplicity.

In using a method which is essentially that of poetry[1] the author was returning, I think, to the practice of the 4th century Quietists, portions of whose apocalyptic utterances are preserved for us in *Chuang Tzŭ*, *Lieh Tzŭ*,

[1] I am not here merely referring to the fact that most of the book is in rhyme: cf. Bernhard Karlgren, *The Poetical Parts in Lao Tsi*, Göteborg, 1932.

Introduction

Kuan Tzŭ and *Hsün Tzŭ*.[1] These early Taoist hymns were however clearly intended chiefly for the initiate. Then followed a period of Taoist expansion and propaganda, giving rise to the method of teaching by fable and anecdote which is typical of the 3rd century. This resource the *Tao Tê Ching* discards entirely. Its aim indeed is not to produce conviction upon any one point or understanding of any particular doctrine, but to create in the reader a general attitude favourable to Quietism. For the art of Tao is in its essence not merely incommunicable (as indeed are all arts) but secret, as is every technique in the pre-scientific world. Nevertheless, as a sort of Masonic sign to initiate readers that the author himself is an initiate, a certain number of passages do allude in a veiled way to the physical technique of Taoism, to breath-control and sexual régime. In such passages—there are not more than four or five of them—there is a double meaning, an esoteric and an exoteric. But the esoteric meaning is not intended to convey information. It is merely as it were a greeting to fellow Taoists into whose hands the book might chance to fall.

The Author

The reader may at this point well ask why I have all this time said nothing about the author of the book. The reason is a simple yet cogent one. There is nothing to say. We do not know and it is unlikely that we shall ever know who wrote the *Tao Tê Ching*. But for two thousand years the name of Lao Tan or 'Master Lao' (Lao Tzŭ) was connected with this book. To understand how this happened

1 P'ien 21.

one needs to know something about the history of authorship in China, and as the subject is a rather complicated
one, I shall discuss it in a separate essay.[1]

Meanwhile, before closing this introduction, I should
like to meet two possible lines of criticism. It may be
said that in my account of early Chinese thought I have
wandered from author to author, picking out a scrap here
or there, and taking no notice of the surrounding context.
My answer is that several of my main sources (*Kuan Tzŭ*,
Han Fei Tzŭ) are in themselves essentially a patchwork, in
that they constantly quote early Quietist rhymes and
maxims, and then proceed to reinterpret them in a Realist
way. It is quite legitimate to divorce the text from the
sermon.

It will certainly be said that my account of the Realists
is coloured by recent events in Europe—that I have
'touched up' the picture, so as to give it the added interest
of topicality. I can only ask anyone who thinks this to read
J. Duyvendak's translation of *Shang Tzŭ*, a work which
came out some five years ago and reads like a prophecy of
recent events in Germany.

[1] Appendix I.

APPENDIX I

Authorship in Early China, and the Relation of the Lao Tan Legend to the 'Tao Tê Ching'

THE EARLIEST use of connected writing (as opposed to isolated magic pictures, developing into magic patterns) was as an aid to memory. That is to say, its purpose was to help people not to forget what they knew already; whereas in more advanced communities the chief use of writing is to tell people things that they have not heard before. Writing in early China, for example, was used to record the taking of omens, in order to assist in the correct interpretation of future omens. It was used to record infrequent rites, such as those of coronation[1] which might occur only once in a generation and were consequently apt to be imperfectly remembered. It was used to record the *libretti* of the great sacrificial dances that attended the worship of dynastic founders,[2] to record the main events (campaigns, reprisals, visits from other tribes, together with portents and omens other than those obtained by divination) of tribal life. All such writing as this was necessarily anonymous. No notion of 'authorship' attended it. It was merely the work of scribes, mechanically setting down things that were in danger of being forgotten.

Then came a time when men were interested in words and thoughts, as well as in actions. There arose a new kind of person, such as Confucius himself, who said

[1] See *Book of History*, Ku Ming.

[2] Such as the Great War Dance celebrating the defeat of the Shang by the Chou. Considerable parts of its *libretto* survive in the *Book of History* and elsewhere.

things that their followers were anxious not to forget. Tzŭ-ch'ang, we know, once wrote down a memorable saying of the Master's upon the lappet of his sash. There is no reason to doubt that the pupils of the early philosophers frequently recorded remarks in this way. Later on such jottings were collected and, along with oral traditions, framed into works such as the *Analects* and *Mencius*. But still there was no notion of 'authorship' in the modern sense of the word. Nor was there any idea that a book must have a title, a fixed name. Take for example the work that Europeans call the *Book of History*. The 'History' part of the title is our invention, and not a very happy one. For no book could be less historical. The early sources generally call it simply *Shu*, 'the writings', or they quote it by the names of individual sections in the work, or else they say 'in the writings of the Chou', 'in the writings of the Hsia', etc.; since then it has had a variety of other names. Nor is this tendency to describe books by any name that seemed to suit their contents confined to early times; there are books that, written long after the Christian era, only arrived at their present titles in the Sung dynasty or later.

Thus people in early China were used to regarding books as records of tradition. Their purpose was to save ancient and venerable things from oblivion. Consequently it was perfectly natural that when real authorship began writers should give their books the appearance of being records of ancient things, rather than present their ideas as new and personal discoveries. This was as natural and as inevitable as that the first railway carriages should imitate stage coaches. These early products of authorship were not, strictly speaking, what Western bibliographers call pseudepigraphs. No pretence was made that the books in question were written by the Ancients (though this was often believed in after ages by people who could only think in terms of modern authorship). It was merely pretended that what was now set down had once been taught by such or such an Ancient. Had this method not been adopted the people could not have been induced to read the books,[1] any more than travellers could have been persuaded to enter a railway carriage if it had not looked something like a stage coach.

Thus in the huge collection of writings known as *Kuan Tzŭ* a great many opinions are put into the mouth of a certain Kuan Chung who is supposed to have been Minister in Ch'i in the 7th century B.C. We should be wholly mistaken, however, if we supposed (as a famous modern scholar has done) that these opinions were such as the 3rd century writers who compiled the book had good reason to accept as Kuan Chung's. It would never have occurred to them to ask, for example, whether iron was really used in Kuan Chung's time. But when they had advice to give about the control of the iron industry (already flourishing in the 3rd century, but almost certainly non-existent in the 7th) they naturally and without a thought put this advice into Kuan Chung's mouth. In the same way the author of *Shang Tzŭ*, who lived in the 3rd century, in order to give weight to his extreme Realist views puts them into the mouth of, or at any rate often appeals to the authority of Shang Yang, a 4th century Minister. Again, a Taoist wrote the *Book of the Yellow*

[1] As is explained by *Chuang Tzŭ*, 27. 1.

Ancestor, now known to us only in quotation. The Yellow Ancestor lived, as we have seen, somewhere about the 4th millennium B.C., being relegated to this remote period because there was no room for him in any other. There was no suggestion that the book was actually written by this fabulous divinity, but only that it embodied his teachings, which had afterwards been handed down orally from generation to generation. And finally the *Tao Tê Ching*, owing to its constant use of sayings which everyone connected with the name of Lao Tan (Lao Tzŭ, the Master Lao), naturally came to be regarded as embodying the teaching of this legendary Quietist. Whether it was definitely put into the world as a record of the teachings of Lao Tan or whether this ascription was merely one that grew up in the minds of readers we cannot know.

Thus in regard to a whole series of Chinese books a rather complicated state of affairs exists, which was completely misunderstood in China until quite recent times, and appears still to be very imperfectly understood by European scholars. In each case we get (1) an ancient Worthy, (2) centuries later, a book 'sheltering itself' (as the Chinese say) under his name. It occurred very early to the Chinese that some of these books were not in point of fact by the ancient worthies in question. But already the conventions of primitive authorship, the ritual of self-effacement that custom imposed upon it, were completely forgotten, and to the medieval Chinese there appeared to be only two alternatives: either the book really was by the Worthy, or else it was by a forger, and therefore must not be read. For forgery is wicked, and nothing useful can be learnt from the books of wicked men. Now such is the spell that the *Tao Tê Ching* has always had over the minds of all save the most narrow and rigid sectaries of Confucianism that so long as no middle way presented itself China has been obliged, despite every evidence to the contrary, to accept the book as a work of a legendary Worthy, Lao Tan; for the only alternative was to admit that it was a forgery, in which case it could not be read. I am speaking, of course, of the ordinary public. In the Taoist Church the book had long ago become a sacred scripture, the authenticity of which it was profanity to question.

In 'fathering' their works upon the Ancients or in issuing them anonymously in such a form that the public would accept them as inspired by the Ancients, early Chinese writers were in point of fact doing nothing disreputable, but merely conforming to the accepted ritual of authorship. Such a view is only just beginning to be accepted in China, and there is still a great deal of confusion between proving (1) that a work is not by its 'sheltering' Worthy, (2) proving that it is not by an anonymous writer of the period when the 'sheltering' ritual still prevailed. Nor is this confusion confined to Chinese works. Thus in trying to prove that *Kuan Tzŭ* is a forgery of the 4th century A.D. a French scholar mentions that in one place *Kuan Tzŭ* adopts the chronology of the State of Lu, 'absurd for a Minister of Ch'i' in the 7th century B.C. If this were true, it would merely prove that *Kuan Tzŭ* is not a work by its 'sheltering' Worthy, Kuan Chung. It would have no bearing whatever on whether *Kuan Tzŭ* is an anonymous work of the 3rd century B.C. or a forgery of the 4th century A.D.

Historicity is a quantitative matter. Queen Victoria

is indubitably an historical character and not a mere
legend. Yet among the things that we believe about her,
some at least are likely to be false. The Cid is mainly
legendary; yet embedded in this legend are certain grains
of fact. The Worthies upon whom the Chinese of the 3rd
century B.C. fathered their books represent varying degrees
of historicity. There is not much doubt that a Ch'i
Minister called Kuan Chung existed at the date alleged;
but we know very little about him. Shang Yang is perfectly historical. The Yellow Ancestor is, I suppose, as
mythical as it is possible to be. Lao Tan, the ancient
Worthy under whose ægis the *Tao Tê Ching* has sheltered,
is hard to classify, being a composite figure, made up of
very heterogeneous elements. I do not intend here to ana-
lyse his legend, inextricably interwoven as it is with that
of another sage called Lao Lai-tzŭ, to a lesser extent with
that of Grandfather P'êng, the Chinese Methusaleh, and
finally with the facts concerning a perfectly historical
personage, also called Lao Tan, who was Treasurer of the
Chou State about 374 B.C. When in the 1st century B.C.
Ssŭ-ma Ch'ien attempted[1] to write a life of Lao Tan
(whom he naturally regarded as the author of the *Tao Tê
Ching*) he found himself confronted, as he confesses, with
a mass of conflicting legend, which he was entirely unable
to disentangle. The information he gives can be analysed
as follows:

1. Birthplace, derived from the Lao Lai Tzŭ legend.

2. Nomenclature (surname, *tzŭ* etc., all complete as

[1] *Shih Chi*, 63.

though he were a T'ang dynasty official), an interpolation, as early quotations show.

3. Rank (Treasurer of Chou), derived from identification of Lao Tan with the 4th century Chou official of the same name. This is, of course, inconsistent with the meeting with Confucius, who lived a century earlier.

4. Story about Lao Tan's meeting with Confucius. An anti-Confucian Taoist legend similar to those in *Chuang Tzŭ* and elsewhere, no more relevant to historical facts than are the Taoist stories of Confucius's discomfiture at the hands of the Brigand Chê.

5. Story of Lao Tan's departure through the Pass. (cf. *Lieh Tzŭ* III. 2.) At the request of the Pass keeper Yin Hsi (also a famous Taoist Worthy) he writes a book in two *p'ien* 'embodying his ideas about *Tao* and *Tê*, and running to somewhat more than 5,000 words'.

6. Question as to whether Lao Tan and Lao Lai Tzŭ are not really the same person (Ssŭ-ma Ch'ien knew that Lao Lai Tzŭ figures instead of Lao Tan in stories about Confucius very similar to the one he has just told.)

7. Records that some people said Lao Tan lived to be 160; while others put the figure at over 200.

8. Quotes an historical reference to the Lao Tan who was Treasurer in 374 B.C., and remarks that though some say he is identical with Lao Tan the philosopher, others say no.

9. Quotes a genealogy by which the Li family in the 2nd century B.C. tried to establish its descent from Lao Tan whom they clearly identify with the historical Treasurer of the 4th century B.C.

10. Reflections on the mutual and quite unnecessary hostility of Taoists and Confucians.

In short, Ssŭ-ma Ch'ien's 'biography' of Lao Tzŭ consists simply of a confession that for the writing of such a biography no materials existed at all.

APPENDIX II.

Foreign Influence

IT HAS often been suggested that the Quietism of early China (4th and 3rd centuries B.C.) was to some extent moulded by Indian influence. It has been suggested that other trends of Chinese thought belonging to the same period[1] were also due to foreign influence. Thus it has been said that the theory of the Five Elements (Wu Hsing) may be connected with the Greek στοιχεῖα. Admittedly the Greek system enumerates the elements differently. But *hsing* means 'to walk', 'to go', and the Greek word for elements means literally 'steps'. It has also been said that the Dualist theory, which divides everything in the universe into the two categories *yin* and *yang*, is derived from Zoroastrianism. Finally, it has been claimed that the conundrums of the language-discriminators or 'sophists' were merely confused echoes of Greek thought.

Here we are only directly concerned with the question of a possible Indian influence on Taoism. The probability of such an influence becomes, however, much stronger if it can be shown that other branches of Chinese thought were being affected by outside influences at the same period. Let us examine these three allegations one by one.

1.—*The Five Elements*

Though *hsing* means 'to walk', 'to go', 'to set in motion',

[1] In common with most scholars in China and Japan I see no reason

'to operate', 'operation', 'conduct' (a man's 'walk' being taken as symbolic of behaviour in general, c.f. our 'walk warily', meaning 'behave with caution'), it never means 'a step'. What was the original sense of *hsing* in this connection? I fancy *Wu hsing* meant the Five Operations, i.e. the operations of the five constituent parts of nature, wood, fire, earth, metal and water. In that case the idea 'element' is not expressed, but understood, and it is irrelevant to compare *hsing* with στοιχεῖον.

2.—*Yin and Yang*

These terms mean literally 'dark side' and 'sunny side' of a hill. Hence, the shady side of anything, as opposed to the side that is in the sun. Suddenly, in a work[1] which is partially of the 4th century B.C. we find these terms used in a philosophical sense. *Yin* and *yang* are categories, corresponding to male and female, weak and strong, dark and light. At the same time they are (though this view has been recently combated) quite definitely forces; for *yin* is the vital-energy (*ch'i*, the life-breath of Earth, just as *yang* is the life-breath of Heaven). The work in question is currently printed in 24 paragraphs; only in three of these are the terms *yin* and *yang* used at all. The division into paragraphs is of course relatively modern, and I only

to place the Five Element theory earlier than the 4th century. The question is too complicated to discuss here.

[1] The *Hsi Tz'ŭ*, Appendix III to the *Book of Changes* in Legge's edition. There is one mention of *yin-yang* in the *Chou Kuan* chapter of the *Book of History*. This chapter is one of those which are generally regarded as the work of a third century A.D. forger.

mention it to show how very small a part these terms play in the Dualist theory. There is however little doubt that they assumed a much more important rôle in the speculations of Tsou Yen,[1] who flourished in Ch'i at the end of the 4th and beginning of the 3rd century B.C.; and they figure considerably in some of the Taoist treatises that form the collections *Chuang Tzŭ* and *Lieh Tzŭ*. It is however an exaggeration to say that 'the theory of *yin* and *yang* spread rapidly. From the end of the 5th century it was generally adopted by all philosophers'.[2] In the *Analects*, which were in process of formation at any rate down till about 350 B.C., there is no mention of *yin* and *yang*. In the works of the Mo Tzŭ school there is only one stray reference. In important Confucian works such as *Mencius*, the *Chung Yung*, the *Ta Hsüeh*, these terms do not occur at all. Out of the 76 surviving *p'ien* of *Kuan Tzŭ* only some half dozen mention *yin* and *yang*. Even in the second half of the 3rd century the Dualist theory was not widely accepted. It had little influence on Hsün Tzŭ or Han Fei Tzŭ. It is utilized in the calendrical parts of the *Lü Shih Ch'un Ch'iu*, but hardly at all in the other parts of this very catholic encyclopædia. Now my purpose in emphasizing the relative unimportance of the Dualist theory during the 4th and 3rd centuries is to explain why it is that the terms *yin* and *yang* figure so sparingly in my account of early Chinese thought, whereas some works on early China, particularly those dealing with archæology,

[1] His works (running to over 100,000 words, according to the *Shih Chi* of Ssŭ-ma Ch'ien) no longer survive; some account of them however is given by the *Shih Chi* in an appendix to the biography of Mencius.

[2] Maspero, *La Chine Antique*, p. 485.

attempt to explain every phenomenon in the light of the *yin-yang* Dualism. I will now return from this short digression, and ask what evidence there is that the Dualist conception was imported from the Iranian world.

In Zoroastrianism Darkness is essentially evil; the principle of Light, essentially good. The fundamental conception of *yin* and *yang* is quite different. They are two interdependent and complementary facets of existence, and the aim of *yin-yang* philosophers was not the triumph of Light, but the attainment in human life of perfect balance between the two principles. I will not here speculate as to how this conception arose in China.[1] In order to do so we should have to examine the whole history of yarrow-stalk divination, the fancies that wove themselves round the properties of the numbers that played important parts in this system of divination, which is essentially a development of primitive omen-taking by 'odds' and 'evens'. Suffice it to say that while it is quite easy to see how the *yin-yang* theory may have grown up out of native divination, it is very difficult indeed to imagine that even the most confused and distorted account of Persian religion could have given rise to the *yin-yang* system as we know it in China.

3.—Greek Influence on the Sophists

Chuang Tzŭ (XXXIII. 7) enumerates themes which were dealt with by the Chinese 'sophists'. Among these three have been supposed to show an affinity with topics discussed by the Greeks.

[1] It is noteworthy that an apparently arbitrary classification of all objects into two or more categories is found among primitives, for example in Australia.

Foreign Influence

a. 'The Tortoise is longer than the snake.' This seems at first sight to be merely a stupid pun on two senses of the *ch'ang*, which means 'long' in time as well as 'long' in space. But to the 'word-discriminators' such inadequacies of language were no joke at all. See above, p. 65. Cumulatively they made effective government impossible. In the present case it is shown that whereas in the world of fact length in time does not necessarily involve length in space, in the world of language no such distinction is made. There is no reason to think that we here have a confused echo of 'Achilles and the Tortoise'.

b. Something about an arrow which, as it stands, makes no sense. It is true that by supplying words which are not there, we can easily make the topic appear to have something to do with the arrow of Zeno; but such a proceeding is quite unscientific. What the proposition probably expressed (judging by similar Chinese propositions) is that all movement is relative. In relation to the earth, the arrow-tip moves; in relation to the shaft of the arrow, it stays still.

c. The proposition about halving a stick, which I have already dealt with above (p. 59). It is another way of stating the problem of Achilles and the tortoise ; but at the same time it belongs entirely to Chinese thought, being merely part of a general demonstration that the world of language is quite a different place from the world of reality. In the latter, infinites do not exist.

In the three cases examined above (the Five Elements,

Yin and Yang, Logic) an outside influence is then not an impossibility; but its existence is far indeed from having been proved. We cannot, therefore, say that the formative period of Chinese Quietism (the 4th century) was one when outside influences on thought were general. On the other hand Quietism developed and expanded during a period when such influences were demonstrably beginning to be of great importance. All scholars are, I think, now agreed that the literature of the 3rd century is full of geographic and mythological elements derived from India.[1] I see no reason to doubt that the 'holy mountain-men' (*shêng-hsien*) described by *Lieh Tzŭ* are Indian *rishi*; and when we read in *Chuang Tzŭ* of certain Taoists who practised movements very similar to the *āsanas* of Hindu *yoga*, it is at least a possibility that some knowledge of the *yoga*-technique which these *rishi* used had also drifted into China. It has been said that merchants, who were undoubtedly the main carriers of information about the outside world, are not likely to have been interested in philosophy. This is a notion derived from a false analogy between East and West. It is quite true that Marco Polo 'songeait surtout à son négoce'. But the same can hardly be said of Indian or Chinese merchants. Buddhist legend, for example, teams with merchants reputedly capable of discussing metaphysical questions; and in China Lü Puwei, compiler of the philosophical encyclopædia *Lü Shih Ch'un Ch'iu*, was himself a merchant. Legend even makes a merchant of Kuan Chung; which at any rate shows that

---

[1] See Maspero, *loc. cit.* 608-609, and Lionel Giles, Two Parallel Anecdotes in Greek and Chinese Sources (i.e. *Lieh Tzŭ*), offprint from the *Bulletin of the School of Oriental Studies*.

philosophy and trade were not currently supposed to be incompatible. I see no reason, then, to doubt that the Chinese technique of self-hypnosis may have been supplemented in the 3rd century, particularly towards its close, by hints from abroad. But we are not at present in a position to prove that this was so.

APPENDIX III.

Taoist Yoga

THAT THE Chinese Quietists practised some form of self-hypnosis no one familiar both with the yoga literature of India (whether Hindu or Buddhist) and with Taoism would, I think, be likely to dispute. Take these three passages from *Chuang Tzǔ*:[1] 'The philosopher Ch'i sat propped upon a stool, his head thrown back, puffing out his breath very gently. He looked strangely dazed and inert, as though only part of him were there at all. "What was happening to you?" asked his disciple Yen Ch'êng, who had been standing at his side. "You seem able to make your body for the time being like a log of wood, your mind like dead embers. What I have just seen leaning against this stool appeared to have no connection with the person who was sitting there before." "You have put it very well," said Ch'i; "when you saw me just now my 'I' had lost its 'me'." '

In the second passage the Quietist ruler is said to sit like a *shih*. This is generally translated 'corpse'; but I think it is much more likely to mean the medium (*shih*) who sits motionless and silent at the sacrifice waiting for the spirit of the Ancestor to descend upon him. In the third passage we are told that on one occasion when Confucius visited Lao Tan he found him 'so inert as hardly to resemble a human being'. 'Confucius waited for a while, but presently feeling that the moment had come for

[1] II. 1, XI. 1, and XXI. 4.

announcing himself addressed Lao Tan saying: "Did my
eyes deceive me or can it really have been so? Just now you
appeared to me to be a mere lifeless block, stark as a log
of wood. It was as though you had no consciousness of
any outside thing and were somewhere all by yourself."
Lao Tan said: "True. I was wandering in the Beginning
of Things." '

That these passages describe some form of self-induced
trance is beyond dispute; and that this trance was closely
akin to the *dhyāna* of the Buddhist is shown by the fact
that the Chinese term for practising *dhyāna* (*tso-ch'an*,[1]
literally 'sitting *dhyāna*') is modelled on the term by which
the old Taoists describe the practice referred to in the
above extracts. The Taoist term in question is *tso-wang*,
'sitting with blank mind' and is defined[2] as: Slackening
limbs and frame, blotting out the senses of hearing and
sight, getting clear of outward forms, dismissing knowledge and being absorbed into That which Pervades
Everything.

The technique of self-hypnosis is often connected with
some form of breath-control. In early Buddhism a state
of trance was induced by concentrating the whole of conscious attention upon the incoming and outgoing breaths.
There were other methods; but this was by far the commonest.[3] It is not certain whether this method was used
in China before the advent of Buddhism. But breath-
control was certainly part of Taoist discipline, of the

[1] Ancient Chinese approximately *dian*.   [2] *Chuang Tzŭ*, VI. 10.
[3] See for example the *Rāhulovāda* of the Majjhima Nikāya, the
Brahmacariya of the Samyutta Nikāya, the *Path of Purity* (Pali Text
Society Translations, No. 17) Pt. II, p. 305 seq. And in Chinese, the
Ta-an-pan Shou-i Ching. Nanjio 681, Takakusu XV. 163.

régime by which the initiate became a *chên-jên* or Purified
One. We have seen above[1] that in one place *Chuang Tzŭ*
condemns physical exercises analogous to the yoga *āsanas*;
but elsewhere (*Chuang Tzŭ* VI. 2) it is said that the breathing of the Sage is not like that of ordinary men: 'He
breathes with every part of him right down to the heels.'
'He keeps the Great Treasure (i.e. the initial life-breath)
intact and uses only the new breath. He sees to it that his
"clarified breath" is daily renewed, his evil breath entirely
eliminated.'[2] The breathing of the Sage, we read in many
passages, must be like that of an infant. Later Taoist
writers[3] go a step further, saying that it must be like that
of a child in the womb. This 'womb-breathing' is the
'essence of breath-control', he who has mastered it can
'cure every disease, expose himself with immunity to
epidemics, charm snakes and tigers, stop wounds from
bleeding, stay under the water or walk upon it, stop
hunger and thirst, and increase his own life-span'. The
beginner draws in a breath through his nose, holds it while
he counts mentally up to 120, and then breathes out
through his mouth. Neither in being inhaled nor exhaled
must the breath be allowed to make any sound. And
more must always be breathed in than is breathed out. A
goose-feather should be put (?) above the nostrils, and
when such proficiency has been reached that the breath is
expelled without causing the feather to tremble, the first
stage of the art may be said to have been mastered. The
counting should then be gradually increased up to a
thousand, at which point the practicant will find himself

[1] p. 44. [2] *Lü Shih Ch'un Ch'iu*, 13.
[3] *Pao P'u Tzŭ*, 4th century A.D. Nei P'ien VIII.

growing daily younger instead of older. . . . 'My great-uncle whenever he was very drunk or the weather was uncomfortably hot, used to jump into a pond and remain at the bottom for as much as a whole day. What enabled him to do this was solely his mastery over the art of breath-closing and womb-breathing.'

It is clear that the above passage deals with the abnormal physiological states which are the aim of the fakir rather than of the *yogi*. The reason for this is not far to seek. The *yoga* element in Chinese religious life had during the past century gradually been absorbed in Buddhism. The earliest Chinese works on Buddhist *yoga* date from the 2nd century A.D.[1] Their terminology is partly derived from that of Taoist *yoga*. Thus *dhyāna* is translated by the word *kuan*, which occurs so often in Taoist texts. *Kuan* means originally to 'watch' for omens,[2] and in the dictionaries it is defined as 'looking at unusual things', as opposed to ordinary seeing or looking. Hence, in accordance with the general 'inward-turning' of Chinese thought and vocabulary, it comes to mean 'what one sees when one is in an abnormal state'; and in Taoist literature it is often practically equivalent to our own mystic word 'Vision'. The root from which *dhyāna* comes has however nothing to do with 'seeing' but means simply 'pondering, meditating'; and it was only because *kuan* already possessed a technical sense closely akin to that of *dhyāna* that

---

[1] Nanjio, 681, attributed to An Shih-kao (fl. 148-170 A.D.), is one of the 30 An Shih-kao works accepted by Tao-an (314-385 A.D.). It has a preface by K'ang Sêng-hui (died 280 A.D.). It is not a translation of an Indian work, but a paraphrase, with commentary. I see no reason to doubt that it belongs to the 2nd century.

[2] See the *Book of Changes*, section 20.

it was chosen as an equivalent, in preference to some such word as *nien*, or *ssŭ*, which are the natural equivalents.

Chinese Quietism, however, though it found a temporary lodging place in the general Buddhist fold, was never entirely at home there. Gradually[1] it detached itself and formed a sect that owed its metaphysic to Mahayana Buddhism and not to Taoism, but which nevertheless eventually became the 'conductor' for exactly the same psychological forces that had in early days expressed themselves in Taoism. This new sect, called Ch'an in China and Zen in Japan, was like Taoism a 'wordless doctrine'. Like Taoism it discarded outward ceremonies, and like Taoism it startled the novice, loosened his sense of 'is' and 'isn't', by conundrums and paradoxes. Thus Zen which has played so great a part in the spiritual life of China and Japan, which is probably destined to exert before long a considerable influence on the West, is psychologically if not doctrinally the heir of 4th and 3rd century Chinese Quietism.

---

[1] Possibly from the 6th, certainly from the 7th century A.D. onward. It is now recognized that the sect was an internal movement in Chinese Buddhism and owed nothing to India. The whole story of Bodhidharma is a late legend, designed to give status and authority to the movement. See Pelliot, *T'oung Pao*, Vol. XXII, p. 253; and Hu Shih, *Wen Ts'un*, Series 3, p. 395 seq.

APPENDIX IV.

Date; Text and Commentaries

THERE ARE two current methods of dating Chinese texts, both of which have their dangers and disadvantages. The first we may call the bibliographical. This consists in searching literature for references to the text we are examining. We may find them in special book-catalogues or in general literature. Or again, we may find quotations from the text in question in books of known date, and thus get a clue as to its period. This method has been extensively used in China since the 18th century. In itself it is a scientific method; but only so long as it is used in a scientific way. In China it has frequently been used in a very unscientific way; and Europeans, hailing the method as congenial to Western ideas of research, have unfortunately borrowed not only the method, but also a most unscientific use of it. Examples of this have been collected by Professor Karlgren in an article on the authenticity of early Chinese texts.[1] I will deal here only with some further aspects of the question that particularly concern the present introduction and translation.

What is a quotation? M. Maspero[2] says that the *Analects* 'quote' a passage of the *Tao Tê Ching* ('Requite ill-feeling with *tê*'). I should say that both works make use of a stock saying. M. Maspero says[3] that *Lieh Tzŭ* is 'quoted' by the *Lü Shih Ch'un Ch'iu* and must therefore be previous. I

---

[1] *Bulletin of the Museum of Far Eastern Antiquities*, No. 1.
[2] *La Chine Antique*, p. 546.   [3] Op. cit. p. 491.

The Way and its Power

should say that there existed a common oral fund of stories about Quietist sages, and that if one author tells two such stories it certainly does not prove that he derived them from a second author who tells the same stories. Again, it is said[1] that the *Analects* of Confucius must be anterior to the *Ta Hsüeh* ('Great Learning') and *Chung Yung* ('Doctrine of the Mean'), 'which quote passages from it'. But if three Reminiscences of the 'Nineties all told the same story about Oscar Wilde, we should not arbitrarily decide that any one of them was 'quoting' the other. We should regard it as probable that all three were drawing on a common stock of Oscar Wilde tradition. Only if one book said 'As Pennell tells us in his Reminiscences', or something of that kind, should we regard the Wilde saying as a literary quotation. But when we examine the four passages in which the *Analects* are 'quoted' in these two books, we find no mention of the source. It is not said 'in the *Analects* it is written' or the like, but at most 'the Master said'.[2] What possible reason have we to suppose that all three books are not drawing on a common stock of tradition, just as in the modern parallel mentioned above? The same is true of the 'quotations' from the *Analects* that Maspero finds in *Chuang Tzŭ*,[3] *Lieh Tzŭ* and *Mencius*. I venture in these instances to express disagreement with M. Maspero, to whose work I owe so much, merely in order to show that the 'bibliographical' method needs to

[1] Op. cit. p. 546.
[2] Moreover, there is only verbal identity in one passage.
[3] *Analects*, XVIII. 5. cf. *Chuang Tzŭ*, IV. 8; the story of the Madman of Ch'u. This is a typical Taoist story, told in a much more complete form by *Chuang Tzŭ*. I hope to deal with this question elsewhere.

be handled scientifically, which in this case means imaginatively; in other words, it must be linked with an effort to reconstruct in our minds the conditions under which early Chinese books were produced.

Apart from quotations, we may find references in general literature (the question of catalogues has been dealt with by Professor Karlgren) to a text we are trying to date. In reference to the *Book of History* and its recovery after the supposed eclipse of learning during the short-lived Ch'in dynasty, the *Ju-lin Chuan*, the 121st chapter in Ssŭ-ma Ch'ien's History, has been often quoted. A *chuan*, as the character with which it is written shows, is a tradition 'passed from person to person'. No doubt in later days it comes to mean merely a written record. But I think it preserved its sense of 'oral tradition' well into the Han dynasty. The *chuan* inserted in *Han Fei Tzŭ* are certainly of this sort; and the *chuan* attached in the Han dynasty to the *History*, *Odes*, etc., were supposed to represent teaching orally handed down in the Confucian schools. If we compare Ssŭ-ma Ch'ien's annalistic sections[1] with the *chuan*, we feel at once that we are in a different world. To my mind it is the difference between written and oral tradition. The accounts of the kingdoms are chiefly founded on written annals; the biographies and most of the other *chuan* are hearsay, in which facts have become transformed, systematized, romanticized in the process of passing from mouth to mouth. True, many of these *chuan* deal with recent events. But it is not one's experience in

[1] Taking them as a whole; but where adequate annalist material was wanting he has been obliged to pad out even these sections with legendary matter. cf. Yao Ming-ta in *Ku Shih Pien* Vol. II (p. 118 seq.).

The Way and its Power

actual life that facts require centuries, or even years, to accomplish the process of turning into fiction, particularly where an atmosphere of excitement prevails. A great deal of excitement attended the recovery of literature in the 2nd century B.C., and I see no reason to accept Ssŭ-ma Ch'ien's description of the finding of the *Book of History*, any more than I should accept offhand a story about the finding of lost books of Livy. Indeed I see no reason to suppose that in his *chuan*, consisting essentially of things 'told by one person to another' and not based on contemporary written annals, Ssŭ-ma Ch'ien was any more critical than the average modern newspaper. It has not been noticed that next door to the story about the recovery of the *History* is one about the transmission of the *Book of Changes*, which is frankly legendary, at any rate in its earlier part. Ssŭ-ma Ch'ien describes the transmission of Confucius's teaching about the *Changes* through nine generations of master and pupil down to a certain Yang Ho, who flourished about 134 B.C. There is not the slightest evidence, however, that the *Book of Changes* was adopted by Confucianism until late in the 3rd century B.C.; and it does not figure on a par with the *Odes*, *History*, etc., as an accepted element of Confucian curriculum till the Han dynasty.[1]

I mention this only to show that the *Ju-lin Chuan* is a mixture of fiction and fact, as is inevitably the case with all works that depend on oral tradition rather than on

[1] As is well known, the passage (*Analects* VII. 16) in which Confucius himself is made to appear as a student of the *Changes* has probably been tampered with. We know that in the Lu version of the *Analects* the passage ran differently and contained no reference to the *Book of Changes*.

annals in which events were recorded one by one, as they occurred.

The alternative method of dating texts is one that we may call 'internal' or 'evolutionary'. Without going beyond the text itself it attempts to fix the point of evolution revealed on the one hand by grammar, vocabulary and pronunciation (as evidenced by rhymes); and on the other by ideas, legends and general range of allusion. The historical study of Chinese grammar was begun by Karlgren in 1920. He showed, for example, that certain laws obeyed almost without exception in the *Analects* have begun to break down in *Mencius*.[1] The historical study of vocabulary is still in its infancy. It is worth pressing much further. Here again Karlgren has been a pioneer. He has shown for example that in early works the word for boat is *chou*, and that the modern word *ch'uan* does not make its appearance till *Chuang Tzŭ*. I have pushed the enquiry a little further and can show that the new word also occurs in *Mo Tzŭ* (P'ien 45), in the *Lü Shih Ch'un Ch'iu* (P'ien 119), in *Han Fei Tzŭ* (P'ien 28), in *Kuan Tzŭ* (P'ien 13), in the *Chan Kuo Ts'ê* (V. 19); it does not however seem to occur in *Hsün Tzŭ*. Broadly speaking, we may say that this word began to come in during the 3rd century and by Han times had definitely replaced *chou* as the general word for a boat. There are no doubt many other words that could be subjected to the same sort of historical analysis. I have collected and hope to publish a few other examples. It will be seen that it ought to be possible ultimately to build up on this principle a very

[1] The same question was treated from a rather different angle by Hu Shih (*Wên Ts'un*, Vol. II).

useful series of word-tests. Karlgren again has dealt with the subject of rhyme, showing for example in his *The Poetical Parts in Lao-tsi* (1932) that the rhyme-system of the *Tao Tê Ching* is typical of the period at which I place the work.

But there exists a species of 'internal' test more important than the purely philological ones just described. I have given an example of it above (p. 93) in connection with the story of the wicked San Mao. As an example of the evolution of beliefs one might take the case of the *hsien* ('mountain-men'), the Immortals of later Taoism. In *Lieh Tzŭ* they are mysterious people who live in a far-off land. There is no suggestion that anyone in China can 'become' a *hsien*. It is not till well into the Han dynasty that to 'turn into a *hsien*' becomes the aim of Taoist asceticism. An example of evolution in legends is supplied by the story of the 'Tyrant' Chou, last ruler of the Yin dynasty. Let us examine the references to him in three works, representing the successive stages in the development of the story. In the *Book of History* (canonical portions only, showing the progress of the legend down to about 500 B.C.) the king drinks excessively, is under the influence of women, sets aside old-established dignitaries and puts scamps in their place, fails to sacrifice to the ancestral-spirits in Heaven, in the conviction that the Divine Right, once given, cannot be forfeited. In the *Lü Shih Ch'un Ch'iu* (showing development in the next 250 years) King Chou not merely drinks excessively but constructs a 'lake of wine'. He is not merely under the influence of women, but commits atrocities in his dealings with them; for example, rips open the belly of a pregnant woman to see what is happening inside. He does not merely set aside the trusted officers of state, but slays them, and flouts Heaven by a whole series of other atrocities, such as putting all his own feudal barons under arrest, and making minced meat of envoys sent from neighbouring lands. The crescendo continues during the Han dynasties, and finally when we reach the *Ti Wang Shih Chi*[1] of Huang-fu Mi (4th century A.D.) the tyrant Chou, though he still cooks envoys, tortures prisoners and feeds his tame tigers on human flesh, has risen to a sort of Satanic grandeur: 'There came a great wind and rain. Oxen and horses were blown off their feet, trees and houses were cast down, a fire from Heaven burnt his palace, for two whole days it blazed, till it was utterly destroyed. But still, though the spirits of the dead wailed and the hills lamented, King Chou was not afraid.'

The above examples are sufficient, I think, to show what an important part the study of the history of thought and the history of legends and myths might play in the dating of early works. Indeed this method, when combined with linguistic tests, is in my view the surest standard; and where literary tradition, as established by bibliographical researches, conflicts with the results of this internal method, I personally am prepared to jetison literary tradition.

Applying these same methods to the *Tao Tê 'Ching* we find that in grammar it is typical of 3rd century B.C. philosophers.[2] In vocabulary there are elements (such as

[1] Now known only in quotation. I am indebted to Ku Chieh-kang for the above account of the expansion of this legend.

[2] Applying Karlgren's nine tests. The only exception is *ssŭ* in the sense of 'thereupon' (Ch. 3). But it occurs in certain fixed combinations of which this (*ssŭ . . . i*) is one.

chiao in Ch. 1 and *chia*, 'fine' in Ch. 31) that point to the latter part of the 3rd century. The rhymes I have already referred to. But it is above all the point of evolution reached by the ideas alluded to in the book that makes its date certain beyond any doubt. It is a controversial work, and the opponents with which it deals did not exist till the 3rd century. There is, moreover (without actual quotation), a continual use of phrases, metaphors and topics derived from *Hsün Tzŭ*, *Han Fei Tzŭ* and the *Lü Shih Ch'un Ch'iu*, or at any rate from sources that these works also used. Failure to realize this fact has made it frequently impossible to extract any meaning from the text, even a purely 'scriptural' one; whereas for anyone who has these contemporary writers in mind very few passages present any difficulty at all. A particularly good example is Chapter 60, the wording of which seems to me to postulate the presence in the author's mind of a whole series of other texts. We have in such cases something vaguely analogous to, but far from identical with, the allusiveness of later Chinese literature. The latter is ornamental; that of the *Tao Tê Ching* is combative and ironical. I have not thought it worth while to tabulate all these correspondences; but many of them will be found in the footnotes and commentary.

Text

The earliest surviving edition of the *Tao Tê Ching* is that of Wang Pi (226-249), an extremely short-lived scholar most of whose life was devoted to the 'scripturalization' of the *Book of Changes*. His text was evidently a very sound one. It has been tampered with here and there; but his commentary was not brought into line with such changes, so that (except in the case of phrases upon which he happened not to comment) we can restore the original reading. We are helped too by the phonetic glosses of Lu Tê-ming (564-635 A.D.).[1] Some time about the 4th century A.D. an unknown Taoist produced what purported to be an independent text, together with what he pretended was a lost Han commentary. It can however easily be shown that this edition is simply the Wang Pi text furnished with a few variants mostly either trivial or erroneous, and a commentary designed to bring the *Tao Tê Ching* into line with contemporary Taoism, which was a very different thing indeed from the Taoism of six hundred years before.

All the commentaries, from Wang Pi's onwards down to the 18th century, are 'scriptural'; that is to say that each commentator reinterprets the text according to his own particular tenets, without any intention or desire to discover what it meant originally. From my point of view they are therefore useless. The 18th century opens up a new era. The study of textual variants begins, and also the historical study of grammar. The latter is of vital importance;[2] the former, as I shall try to show, has not in the case of this particular work, achieved results com-

---

[1] Wang Pi's commentary is rather corrupt and so is Lu Tê-ming's work. But both are adequately serviceable for the purpose in view. The interpretations of passages from the *Tao Tê Ching* to be found in *Han Fei Tzŭ* and *Huai-nan Tzŭ* can also be regarded as partial commentaries.

[2] Cf. Wang Sung-nien's little treatise on the conjunction *yen* in *Tu Shu Tsa Chih*, Yü P'ien, fol. 16.

mensurable with the vast amount of labour expended
upon it.

Variant readings, in such a case, are only of value if they
go back to a source which is surer and better than the text
we already possess. The variants collected by scholars
from Pi Yüan in the 18th century down to Ma Hsü-lun
in our own day are of two classes. The first is drawn from
quotations of the *Tao Tê Ching* in early works. These
quotations are always short, and judging from every
known analogy we may presume that they were made
from memory. In our own books Shakespeare, Keats, the
Bible are constantly misquoted. Why should we repose a
vast faith in the accuracy of early Chinese quotations? If
there were a case where the original was hopelessly corrupt
and an early writer quoted a version that not merely
looked convincing but gave us some inkling of how the
corruption arose, then we should be justified in bringing
the text into line with the quotation. But no such case·
exists. In the few places where the text is obviously corrupt the variants are, in my opinion, simply more or less
intelligent suggestions,[1] such as we could perfectly well
make for ourselves. There is not the slightest evidence
that any single variant based on an early quotation really
goes back to an independent and better text. In one case a
quotation—that of the 6th century commentary on the
Shih Shuo Hsin Yü—supplies a smooth and easy version of a
sentence which in the text as we have it (Ch. 13) is hard to

[1] The variants in *Han Fei Tzŭ* and *Huai-nan Tzŭ* are hardly of this
class. Both books are interpreting the text in a manner so totally
divorced from its original meaning that they end, so it seems to me,
by becoming somewhat reckless even concerning the wording of the
text itself. Both, too, were probably quoting from memory.

construe. Here again, it is unlikely in the extreme that
the commentator rushed to a copy of the *Tao Tê Ching* in
order to quote a single sentence. He quoted from memory, and his memory unconsciously smoothed out and
simplified the difficult clause. It is far wiser to make the
best we can of the text as it stands, rather than use this
probably quite unintentional emendation.

So much for quotations. There remains the question of
early texts. Several times during the T'ang dynasty the
Tao Tê Ching was engraved on stone, and some of these
slabs still survive. All of them follow the spurious 4th
century text, embellishing it with a great variety of small
emendations and simplifications. Where these merely
concern unessential particles they become little more than
a matter of 'typography' and need not detain us. Their
efforts to 'make better sense' of the original are almost
always connected with the fact that the whole context
meant something quite different to them from what was
intended by the author. This also holds good of the
T'ang MSS. recovered from Tun-huang,[1] which include
at least one partial Wang Pi version. Their emendations
are either negligible or are due simply to misunderstand-
ing. As to Sung, Yüan and Ming texts—it seems to me
pure waste of time to tabulate all their small differences.

Checked by Lu Tê-ming's glosses and the Wang Pi
commentary, our text is at least as satisfactory as that of
other early Chinese works. Occasionally modern writing
conventions require us to alter a determinative; in one or
two instances we have to take a reading from the 'spurious' text; for it and the Wang Pi text have to some slight

[1] Now in the British Museum and Bibliothèque Nationale.

extent become mutually contaminated. Of actual emendations really affecting the sense I have made only one, consisting in the omission of a single negative; and in this case it is easy to see how the corruption arose.

APPENDIX V

The Formation of Chinese Pre-history

THE GRADUAL rise of the idea of empire, of a great State 'without rival under Heaven' was accompanied by the theory that the Ancestors had ruled over such an Empire. In actual fact, however, the Chinese knew practically nothing about their own past previous to the 8th century B.C. Tradition indeed said that from the 11th to the 9th century the Chou had exercised a sort of glorified hegemony far more complete than those actually witnessed in the historic period. We have no reason to reject this tradition altogether; but what the extent of this hegemony was, whether it was mainly cultural or also political, we do not know and certainly cannot discover except through archæological finds.[1] As for the Yin, the ancient Chinese knew nothing about them except the names of their kings. To-day, owing to the discovery of the Honan oracle bones (11th century B.C.), we know something about the life and preoccupations of the Yin people; but nothing that can be called history.

European writers, not understanding the process by which Chinese prehistorical chronology was built up, have till recently been apt to assume that, even if such figures as the Yellow Ancestor (Huang Ti) whom this chronology

[1] A certain amount of information can be gleaned from archæological evidence already existing; for example, from inscriptions on bronzes. But the pitfalls in such a line of research are obviously numerous. The best collection of inscriptions is Kuo Mo-jo's *Liang Chou Chin Wên Tzǔ Ta Hsi*, Tōkyō, 1932.

places in the 3rd millennium B.C.) are legendary, the stories told about them do actually reflect the state of culture in China during the third millennium or at any rate during a very early period. Legend, for example, says that the Yellow Ancestor cast nine bronze tripods; therefore even if the Ancestor is mythical (so this argument runs) we may at least conclude that the use of metal was known thousands of years before history. Such an argument would not be used if it were understood that the Yellow Ancestor was put into this remote period by the chronologists merely in just the same way as someone arriving late at a crowded concert is put at the back of the room. Each Chinese tribe had at the outset its own ancestral cult and ancestral mythology. The establishment of successive hegemonies brought about a constant merging of ancestral cults. So long as Ancestors (such as Yao, Shun, the Great Yü) were conceived of merely as Former Kings of a particular tribe, they could exist in popular imagination side by side, floating in a vague past. But when the idea of Empire arose, and it was asserted as a justification of an Imperialist policy that the Chou, for example, once ruled over everything under Heaven, having conquered the Yin who also ruled the world, it was no longer possible to place a mighty and venerated Ancestor such as Yao at the same period as the Yin or Chou 'Empires', and thus make him a subject of Yin or Chou. To bring him down to the historical period was obviously impossible, and the only alternative was to give him the vacant space previous to the dominance of the Yin. Yao and Shun do not appear in the earliest literature and still figure very dimly in the *Analects*. The Yellow Ancestor

The Formation of Chinese Pre-history

was an even later comer, and had consequently to be accommodated 'behind' Yao, in an even more remote corner of prehistory. Thus the chronology was built up backwards, and has no relation whatever with an actual time-sequence.

APPENDIX VI

Sources of Doubtful Date

Kuan Tzŭ

B. KARLGREN has shown (*Bulletin of the Museum of Far Eastern Antiquities*, No. 1) that none of the 'bibliographical' arguments which would relegate *Kuan Tzŭ* to the 3rd or 4th century A.D. are valid. Internal evidence for the 3rd century B.C. as the date for this work as a whole is overwhelming. See Lo Kên-tsê, *Ku Shih Pien*, IV. 615. Certain parts are older; see Haloun, *Asia Major*, IX. 3 (1933).

Lieh Tzŭ

European opinion (Karlgren, Maspero) tends (quite rightly) to put *Lieh Tzŭ* in the 3rd century B.C.; but it seems as though Ma Hsü-lun's 'Doubts about the Authenticity of *Lieh Tzŭ*' (written some 14 years ago) still holds the field in China. None of the arguments used by Ma Hsü-lun and his supporters are of a kind that I can regard as in any way valid, and internal evidence points to the 3rd century B.C. for a large part of the contents.

Han Fei Tzŭ

It is agreed that the chapters in this collection fall into three classes: (1) those which are certainly by Han Fei himself, (2) those which show strong affinity in style and content with the Han Fei chapters, (3) the rest.

Two chapters form a sort of commentary on parts of the *Tao Tê Ching*, interpreting it (in a very forced way) according to a syncretist philosophy in which Taoism and Realism both play a part. It has never been suggested that these chapters belong to class (1) or (2). If anyone succeeded in proving that they were by Han Fei himself, we should know that they were earlier than 235, the date of his death. Various other problems would arise, so hypothetical that they need not here be dealt with.

Chan Kuo Ts'ê

Is the débris of a work composed in the early years of the Han dynasty? For the question of its authorship, see *Ku Shih Pien*, IV. 229.

K'ung Tzŭ Chia Yü

In order to establish this book as part of the Confucian curriculum, Wang Su (3rd century A.D.) provided it with forged credentials. The idea, however, that the work we possess is not part of that which circulated in Han times, is quite unfounded. Wang Su may have tampered with certain passages. But this cannot often be the case; for there are only ten paragraphs in the whole book which have not (as regards content, though not as regards phrasing) exact parallels in early literature. A list of most of these parallels is given by Gustav Haloun in *Asia Major* VIII. fascicule 3, where the inadequacy of the usual arguments against the authenticity of the *Chia Yü* is shown. The Chinese were faced with the alternative of regarding the *Chia Yü* as a late forgery or of accepting its *logia* as genuine utterances of Confucius. For us this dilemma does not exist. The *Chia Yü* represents the Confucian legend as it developed during the 3rd century B.C.

TAO TÊ CHING

TAO TÊ CHING

CHAPTER I

The Way that can be told of is not an Unvarying Way;
The names that can be named are not unvarying names.
It was from the Nameless that Heaven and Earth sprang;
The named is but the mother that rears the ten thousand
creatures, each after its kind.
Truly,[1] 'Only he that rids himself forever of desire can see
the Secret Essences';
He that has never rid himself of desire can see only the
Outcomes.[1]
These two things issued from the same mould, but never-
theless are different in name.
This 'same mould' we can but call the Mystery,
Or rather the 'Darker than any Mystery',
The Doorway whence issued all Secret Essences.

Paraphrase

The Realists demand a *ch'ang-tao*, an 'unvarying way' of
government, in which every act inimical and every act
beneficial to the State is codified and 'mated' to its
appropriate punishment or reward. The Taoist replies
that though there does exist a *ch'ang-tao*,[2] 'an unvarying

[1] See additional notes.   [2] *Han Fei Tzu*, 51.

Way', it cannot be grasped by the ordinary senses nor described in words. In dispassionate vision the Taoist sees a world consisting of the things for which language has no names. Provisionally we may call them *miao*, 'secret essences'. The Realist, his vision distorted by desire, sees only the 'ultimate results', the Outcomes of those essences, never the essences themselves. The whole doctrine of Realism was founded on the conviction that just as things which issue from the same mould are mechanically identical, 'cannot help being as they are',[1] so by complete codification, a series of moulds (*fa*), can be constructed, which will mechanically decide what 'name' (and consequently what reward or punishment) should be assigned to any given deed. But the two modalities of the Universe, the world as the Taoist sees it in vision and the world of everyday life, contradict the basic assumption of the Realist. For they issue from the same mould ('proceed from a sameness'), and nevertheless are different as regards name. Strictly speaking, the world as seen in vision has no name. We can call it, as above, the Sameness; or the Mystery. These names are however merely stop-gaps. For what we are trying to express is darker than any mystery.

---

[1] *Kuan Tzŭ*, 36, just after middle.

CHAPTER II

IT IS because every one under Heaven recognizes beauty as beauty, that the idea of ugliness exists.
And equally if every one recognized virtue as virtue, this would merely create fresh conceptions of wickedness.
For truly 'Being and Not-being grow out of one another;
Difficult and easy complete one another.
Long and short test[1] one another;
High and low determine one another.
Pitch and mode give harmony to one another.
Front and back give sequence to one another .
Therefore[2] the Sage relies on actionless activity,
Carries on wordless teaching,
But the myriad creatures are worked upon by him; he does not disown them.
He rears them, but does not lay claim to them,
Controls them, but does not lean upon them,
Achieves his aim, but does not call attention[3] to what he does;
And for the very reason that he does not call attention to what he does
He is not ejected from fruition of what he has done.

Paraphrase

The Realists say that virtue (i.e. what the State desires)

[1] See textual notes.
[2] Because 'action' can only make one thing high at the expense of making something else low, etc.
[3] Lit.: 'does not place (i.e. classify) himself as a victor'. cf. *Mencius*, II. 1. 2. 19.

must, by complete codification, be made as easily recognizable as beauty. When people see Hsi Shih (the legendary paragon of beauty) they at once know that she is the most beautiful of women; but when they see good men (i.e. those who are strong-limbed but docile, see *Shang Tzŭ*) they mistake them for boors. This can only be avoided if the State clearly labels the good as good.

But, says the Taoist, by admitting the conception of 'goodness' you are simultaneously creating a conception 'badness'. Nothing can be good except in relation to something that is bad, just as nothing can be 'in front' except in relation to something that is 'behind'. Therefore the Sage avoids all positive action, working only through the 'power' of Tao, which alone 'cuts without wounding', transcending all antinomies.

The type of the Sage who in true Taoist manner 'disappeared' after his victory is Fan Li[1] (5th century B.C.) who, although offered half the kingdom if he would return in triumph with the victorious armies of Yüeh, 'stepped into a light boat and was heard of no more'.

---

[1] *Kuo Yü*, 21. The passage is closely akin to the *Tao Tê Ching* both in language and thought.

CHAPTER III

IF WE stop looking for 'persons of superior morality' (*hsien*) to put in power, there will be no more jealousies among the people. If we cease to set store by products that are hard to get, there will be no more thieves. If the people never see such things as excite desire, their hearts will remain placid and undisturbed. Therefore the Sage rules

By emptying their hearts (decreasing desires, making pure & simple)
And filling their bellies,
Weakening their intelligence[1]
And toughening their sinews
Ever striving to make the people knowledgeless and
    desireless.

Indeed he sees to it that if there be any who have knowledge, they dare not interfere. Yet through his actionless activity all things are duly regulated.

Commentary
(anti-Confucius)

This chapter is a bait for Realists. The author shows that like them he is against the raising of *hsien*, is against knowledge, trade, luxury, etc. But he slips in *wu-yü*, desireless (see Introduction, p. 89) and *wu-wei*, 'non-activity', i.e. rule through *tê* ('virtue', 'power') acquired in trance.

Make it sound like Lao Tzu is a realist, but he's really opposed & showing how someone should learn

[1] Particularly in the sense of 'having ideas of one's own'.

CHAPTER IV

The Way is like an empty vessel
That yet may be drawn from
Without ever needing to be filled.
It is bottomless; the very progenitor of all things in the world.
In it all sharpness is blunted,
All tangles untied,
All glare tempered,
All dust[1] smoothed.
It is like a deep pool that never dries.
Was it too the child of something else? We cannot tell.
But as a substanceless image[2] it existed before the Ancestor.[3]

world arises from emptiness
Its all arising in within & from being

[1] Dust is the Taoist symbol for the noise and fuss of everyday life.

[2] A *hsiang*, an image such as the mental images that float before us when we think. See Introduction, p. 61.

[3] The Ancestor in question is almost certainly the Yellow Ancestor who separated Earth from Heaven and so destroyed the Primal Unity, for which he is frequently censured in *Chuang Tzŭ*.

CHAPTER V

Heaven and Earth are ruthless;
To them the Ten Thousand Things are but as straw dogs.
The Sage too is ruthless;
To him the people are but as straw dogs.
Yet[1] Heaven and Earth and all that lies between
Is like a bellows
In that it is empty, but gives a supply that never fails.
Work it, and more comes out.
Whereas the force of words[2] is soon spent.
Far better is it to keep what is in the heart.[3]

Commentary

Jên, which I have here translated 'ruth' and elsewhere 'gentle', 'kind', etc., is cognate to *jên* 'man'. I believe that *jên* did not originally mean mankind in general, but the members of one's own tribe or group, for whom one has feelings of 'nearness'. (The *Shuo Wên* defines *jên* as *ch'in*, 'akin', 'near'.)

Compare the origin of 'kind' from 'kin' and 'gentle' from *gens*, Latin for a clan. Hence (because members of one's own ethnic group are better than members of other groups) 'good' in the most general sense. In the *Book of*

[1] Though ruthless (as the Realists never tired of maintaining), nature is perpetually bounteous.

[2] Laws and proclamations.

[3] For *chung* as 'what is within the heart', see *Tso Chuan*, Yin Kung 3rd year and *Kuan Tzŭ*, 37, beginning. The comparison of Heaven and Earth to a bellows is also found in *Kuan Tzŭ* (P'ien 11, beginning).

Odes, jên only occurs coupled with *mei*—'handsome and good', i.e. true member of the tribe both in appearance and character. In early Confucianism *jên* acquires a mystic sense, 'The Highest Good', and comes near to playing the part that the term Tao plays in Quietist terminology.

It is to be noted that in the earliest literature (e.g. *Odes* Nos. 249, 256, 257; *Book of History,* Hung Fan) *jên,* 'men of rank', 'men of the tribe' are contrasted with *min,* 'subjects', 'the common people'.

CHAPTER VI

The Valley Spirit never dies.
It is named the Mysterious Female.
And the Doorway of the Mysterious Female
Is the base from which Heaven and Earth sprang.
It is there within us all the while;
Draw upon it as you will, it never runs dry.[1]

[1] For these six lines see Introduction, p. 57. *Lieh Tzŭ* quotes them
as coming from the *Book of the Yellow Ancestor*; but it does not follow
that the *Tao Tê Ching* is actually quoting them from this source. They
may belong to the general stock of early Taoist rhymed teaching For
ch'in compare below, p. 206, line 9, and *Huai-nan Tzu* I, fol. 2.

CHAPTER VII

Heaven is eternal, the Earth everlasting.
How come they to be so? It is because they do not foster
    their own lives;
That is why they live so long.
Therefore the Sage
Puts himself in the background; but is always to the fore.
Remains outside; but is always there.
Is it not just because he does not strive for any personal end
That all his personal ends are fulfilled?

CHAPTER VIII

THE HIGHEST good is like that of water.[1] The goodness of
water is that it benefits the ten thousand creatures; yet
itself does not scramble, but is content with the places
that all men disdain. It is this that makes water so near
to the Way.

And if men think the ground the best place for building a
    house upon,
If among thoughts they value those that are profound,
If in friendship they value gentleness,
In words, truth; in government, good order;
In deeds, effectiveness; in actions, timeliness——
In each case it is because they prefer what does not lead
    to strife,[2]
And therefore does not go amiss.

[1] For water as a Taoist symbol see Introduction, p. 56.
[2] Even ordinary people realize the importance of the Taoist principle of 'water-like' behaviour, i.e. not striving to get on top or to the
fore.

CHAPTER IX

Stretch a bow[1] to the very full,
And you will wish you had stopped in time;
Temper a sword-edge to its very sharpest,
And you will find it soon grows dull.
When bronze and jade fill your hall
It can no longer be guarded.
Wealth and place breed insolence
That brings ruin in its train.
When your work is done, then withdraw!
Such is Heaven's[2] Way.

---

[1] The expression used can also apply to filling a vessel to the brim;
but 'stretching a bow' makes a better parallel to 'sharpening a sword'.
[2] As opposed to the Way of man.

CHAPTER X

Can you keep the unquiet[1] physical-soul from straying,
   hold fast to the Unity, and never quit it?
Can you, when concentrating your breath, make it soft
   like that of a little child?
Can you wipe and cleanse your vision of the Mystery till
   all is without blur?
Can you love the people and rule the land, yet remain
   unknown?
Can you in opening and shutting the heavenly gates play
   always the female part?[2]
Can your mind penetrate every corner of the land, but you
   yourself never interfere?
Rear them, then, feed them,
Rear them, but do not lay claim to them.
Control them, but never lean upon them;
Be chief among them, but do not manage them.
This is called the Mysterious Power.

Commentary

For other versions of the old Taoist hymn which the
author here adapts to his own use, see *Chuang Tzŭ*,
XXIII. 3, and *Kuan Tzŭ* 37 (near beginning). For the
physical-soul or *p'o* see Introduction, p. 28. But as we
have seen *p'o* literally means semen, and there is here an
allusion to a technique of sexual hygiene parallel to

1 See textual notes.
2 Read *wei*, not *wu*. This is the original Wang Pi reading, as the
commentary shows.

breathing technique. For the necessity of soft breathing, see Appendix III. The female (i.e. passive) opening and shutting of the heavenly gates also refers to the opening and shutting of mouth and nostrils. This however was a mildly esoteric meaning; the completely uninitiated would take it in the sense: 'Handle the weightiest affairs of state', as indeed does Wang Pi, the earliest commentator.

Huai-nan Tzŭ (Ch. XII) is quite aware that the opening passage of this chapter deals with the technique of Taoist *yoga*, for in illustration of it he quotes the story (*Chuang Tzŭ*, VI. end) of Yen Hui and his practice of *tso-wang*, 'sitting with blank mind'. See Appendix III.

The phrase *pao-i* or *chih-i* ('holding to the Unity') has a curious history, very typical of the way in which the various schools while retaining the same time-hallowed watchwords, apted them to their own needs. In *Mencius* (VII. 1. 26) it means having a 'one-sided' view, and is the opposite of *chih-chung*, 'holding to the middle' between two extremes. In Quietist language it has a metaphysical sense, meaning to 'hold fast to' the One as opposed to the Many, to utilize the primal, 'undivided' state that underlies the normal consciousness. Finally, to the Realists the phrase meant to maintain the ruler's or the State's absolute, undivided sway. Writers such as Kuan Tzŭ, who base their Realism on a mystic foundation, pass bewilderingly from the Quietist to the political application of the phrase, often seeming to attach both meanings to it simultaneously.

CHAPTER XI

We put thirty spokes together and call it a wheel;
But it is on the space where there is nothing that the
usefulness of the wheel depends.
We turn clay to make a vessel;
But it is on the space where there is nothing that the
usefulness of the vessel depends.
We pierce doors and windows to make a house;
And it is on these spaces where there is nothing that the
usefulness of the house depends.
Therefore just as we take advantage of what is, we should
recognize the usefulness of what is not.

CHAPTER XII

The five colours confuse the eye,
The five sounds dull the ear,
The five tastes spoil the palate.
Excess of hunting and chasing
Makes minds go mad.
Products that are hard to get
Impede their owner's movements.
Therefore the Sage
Considers the belly not the eye.[1]
Truly, 'he rejects that but takes this'.[2]

Commentary

This is an answer to the Hedonists; see Introduction, p. 39. Any attempt to exploit to the full the use of the senses leads to a dulling of those senses. There is a proverb 'Poverty does not impede movement' (cf. *Yen T'ieh Lun*, XVI); whereas riches do, because they tempt bandits to attack. This is sometimes interpreted in a moral sense: 'Poverty is no impediment to (virtuous) courses.' I do not think that the moral sense of *hsing* is intended here.

[1] The belly in this instance means 'what is inside him', his own inner powers.
[2] For this use of 'that' and 'this' (i.e. the world outside and the powers within oneself) cf. *Kuan Tzŭ*, 36, middle.

CHAPTER XIII

'FAVOUR AND disgrace goad as it were to madness;[1] high rank hurts keenly as our bodies hurt.' What does it mean to say that favour and disgrace goad as it were to madness? It means[2] that when a ruler's subjects[3] get it[4] they turn distraught, when they lose it they turn distraught. That is what is meant by saying favour and disgrace goad as it were to madness. What does it mean to say that high rank hurts keenly as our bodies hurt? The only reason that we suffer hurt is that we have bodies; if we had no bodies, how could we suffer? Therefore we may accept the saying: 'He who in dealing with the empire regards his high rank as though it were his body is the best person to be entrusted with rule; he who in dealing with the empire loves his subjects as one should love one's body is the best person to whom one can commit the empire.

Commentary

In this chapter the author takes a number of Individualist (Yang Chu school) sayings and adapts them to his own use. Every individual must devote himself to the perfection of his own life, regardless of outside opinion. 'High rank is greatly detrimental to your (jo) body', i.e. to your self-perfection. Such, I think, is the original meaning of this sentence. But our author is at constant war with this 'self first' school, and by taking jo not as 'your' but in its alternative sense 'like', 'as', he extracts the meaning:

[1] See additional notes. [2] See textual notes. [3] *Hsia.* [4] i.e. favour.

'High rank hurts even as the body hurts'. For the body, the self, which in Yang Chu's doctrine must be put before everything else, is in fact (our author points out) the source of all pain. But so long as we regard the body in this light we can accept the Individualist saying:[1] 'Only he who in dealing with the empire makes the perfection of his own body (i.e. self, life) the primary consideration, may be entrusted with rule. Only he who cares for his own body is fit to govern an empire'—reinterpreting it however as meaning that he must regard his own high position just as he regards his body, that is to say, as the potential source of pain; and he must regard his subjects in the same light.

In *kuei i shên, ai i shên* the *i* has a limiting force. Compare *Analects*, I, 5. 'He must employ the people only at the proper times', and not when they have work to do in the fields. For the Buddhist interpretation of this passage, see additional notes.

---

[1] Cf. in the summary of Individualism in *Lü Shih Ch'un Ch'iu*, P'ien 7: 'He alone may be entrusted with empire who does not let empire interfere with his own life-culture'. *Chuang Tzŭ* (XI. 1. and XXVIII. 1) adapts similar sayings.

CHAPTER XIV

Because the eye gazes but can catch no glimpse of it,[1]
It is called elusive.
Because the ear listens but cannot hear it,[1]
It is called the rarefied.
Because the hand feels for it but cannot find it,
It is called the infinitesimal.
These three, because they cannot be further scrutinized,
Blend into one.
Its rising brings no light;
Its sinking, no darkness.
Endless the series of things without name
On the way back to where there is nothing.
They are called shapeless shapes;
Forms without form;
Are called vague semblances.
Go towards them, and you can see no front;
Go after them, and you see no rear.
Yet by seizing on the Way that was
You can ride[2] the things that are now.
For to know what once there was,[3] in the Beginning,
This is called the essence[4] of the Way.

---

[1] This is the traditional description of ghosts and spirits (cf.
Doctrine of the Mean, paragraph 16) adopted as a description of the Way.
[2] i.e. dominate.
[3] Macrocosmically, in the Universe. Microcosmically, in oneself.
[4] Literally, main-thread.

CHAPTER XV

Of old those that were the best officers of Court
Had inner natures subtle, abstruse, mysterious, penetrating,
Too deep to be understood.
And because such men could not be understood
I can but tell of them as they appeared to the world:
Circumspect they seemed, like one who in winter crosses
    a stream,
Watchful, as one who must meet danger on every side.
Ceremonious, as one who pays a visit;
Yet yielding, as ice when it begins to melt.
Blank, as a piece of uncarved wood;
Yet receptive as a hollow in the hills.
Murky, as a troubled stream——
Which of you can assume such murkiness, to become in
    the end still and clear?
Which of you can make yourself inert,[1] to become in the
    end full of life and stir?
Those who possess this Tao do not try to fill themselves to
    the brim,
And because they do not try to fill themselves to the brim
They are like a garment that endures all wear and need
    never be renewed (?).

Commentary

Jung (appearance, attitude, 'how they appeared to the
world') is a technical term with a long history. In fulfill-
ing religious rites it is not sufficient merely to say the

[1] Text doubtful. It is better to omit *chiu*.

right words or perform the right actions. Each rite requires also an appropriate 'attitude', one of reverence,
eagerness, reluctance, joy, gloominess, etc. These 'attitudes' are always defined in Chinese by quasi-onomato-
pæic words, rather of the 'cock-a-hoop' type; they are
often reduplicatives, and are always followed by an ex-
clamatory or adverbial particle. Among the Confucians
the study of correct attitudes was a matter of prime importance. The *Analects* (especially Book X) constantly
defines these attitudes, and mnemonic jingles were current, in which a whole string of *jung* were connected into
a sort of didactic poetry. The literature of the 3rd century
B.C. teems with *jung*, modelled on those of the ritualists,
but often defining a correct attitude towards life in
general, rather than one appropriate to a particular
ceremony. Thus in *Chuang Tzǔ*[1] we find a *jung* of the
ancient *chên-jên* (Taoist adept, 'perfected, purified man'),
and another[2] of the possessor of 'power', *tê*. The *Lü Shih
Ch'un Ch'iu*[3] gives a *jung* of the perfect State officer, rather
on Taoist lines. *Hsün Tzǔ* has general *jung*, like that of the
'perfect gentleman'[4] and the Sage;[5] but also a more ritualistic definition of the attitudes to be adopted by fathers
and elder brothers, sons and younger brothers, and finally
by pupils in relation to their masters.

The 'which of you can assume murkiness . . . to be
clear' is a *fan-yen*, a paradox, reversal of common speech.
Thus 'the more you clean it the dirtier it becomes' is a
common saying, applied to the way in which slander
'sticks'.[6] But the Taoist must apply the paradoxical rule:
'The more you dirty it, the cleaner it becomes.'

[1] VI. 2.   [2] XII. 12.   [3] P'ien 79   [4] P'ien 3.   [5] P'ien 8.
[6] *Hsün Tzǔ*, P'ien 4 and P'ien 27.

CHAPTER XVI

Push far enough towards the Void,
Hold fast enough to Quietness,
And of the ten thousand things none but can be worked on by
you.
I have beheld them, whither they go back.
See, all things howsoever they flourish
Return to the root from which they grew.
This return to the root is called Quietness;
Quietness is called submission to Fate;
What has submitted to Fate has become part of the always-so.
To know the always-so is to be Illumined;
Not to know it, means to go blindly to disaster.
He who knows the always-so has room in him for everything;
He who has room in him for everything is without prejudice.
To be without prejudice is to be kingly;
To be kingly is to be of heaven;
To be of heaven is to be in Tao.
Tao is forever and he that possesses it,
Though his body ceases, is not destroyed.

Commentary

To have room in one for everything (*jung*) is cognate
both in writing and etymology with 'to be without prejudice' (*kung*). But *kung* happens also to mean a royal Duke,
the person next in rank to the king. There is here a play
on these two senses of *kung*. That the resemblance of two
words may be due to a series of phonological accidents is a

conception that is quite recent in the history of thought. All early thinkers, including the Greeks,[1] attributed a profound significance to such resemblances. *Kung*, then, is a sort of king. And kings are, as has been thought all over the world, delegates of Heaven. Heaven in our author's thought is synonymous with Tao. Tao is the absolute, the enduring, the ever-so.

Such a passage, depending on rhyme, plays on words and resemblance of characters, is of course bound to appear pointless in translation.

---

[1] With the exception of certain rare passages, such as Plato's *Timaeus* (38 b) where rather irrelevantly, in a sort of parenthesis, and in a work which teems with plays on words, it is noted that the verb to be has two uses (1) as a connecting word, (2) meàning 'to exist'; more generally, Hermogenes says in the *Cratylus* (384 D and E) he 'cannot believe' that names are otherwise than conventional.

CHAPTER XVII

Of the highest[1] the people merely know that such a one
    exists;
The next they draw near to and praise.
The next they shrink from, intimidated; but revile.
Truly, 'It is by not believing people that you turn them
    into liars'.[2]
But from the Sage it is so hard at any price to get a
    single word[3]
That when his task is accomplished, his work done,
Throughout the country every one says 'It happened of
    its own accord'.

[1] i.e. most Taoist.
[2] The same saying is quoted in Ch. 23. Cf. Ch. 49: 'The truthful man I believe; but the liar I also believe, and so he (the liar) gets truthfulness.' Similarly it is 'lack' in the ruler which creates in the people every other fault and crime.
[3] Literally: 'How, reluctant, he raises the price of his words!'

CHAPTER XVIII

It was when the Great Way declined
That human kindness and morality arose;
It was when intelligence and knowledge appeared
That the Great Artifice began.
It was when the six near ones[1] were no longer at peace
That there was talk of 'dutiful sons';[2]
Nor till fatherland was dark with strife
Did we hear of 'loyal slaves'.[3]

---

[1] Father, son, elder brother, younger brother, husband and wife.
[2] Read *tzŭ* 'son' not *tz'ŭ* 'compassionate', as in the *Yung Lo Ta Tien* text.
[3] As Ministers called themselves.

CHAPTER XIX

Banish wisdom, discard knowledge,
And the people will be benefited a hundredfold.
Banish human kindness, discard morality,
And the people will be dutiful and compassionate.
Banish skill, discard profit[1],
And thieves and robbers will disappear.
If when these three things are done[2] they find life too
    plain and unadorned,
Then let them have accessories;
Give them Simplicity to look at, the Uncarved Block to
    hold,
Give them selflessness and fewness of desires.

Commentary

For *jên* (human kindness) see above, p. 147. For *i* (morality) see Introduction, p. 66. The virtues which the author here discards were also discarded by the Realists, who maintained that loyalty, for example, may exist in exceptional people, but is absent in most; whereas the love of gain exists in everyone. Consequently, government should be based solely on a complete system of punishments and rewards. The Taoist ruler, on the other hand, creates in his subjects the qualities and tendencies that he desires solely by the exercise of the *tê* that Tao confers.

[1] i.e do away with skilful artisans and enterprising traders, who supply things likely to attract thieves.

[2] I suspect that a negative has fallen out in front of 'these three', and that the original ran: 'If without these three . . . they find life, etc.'

166

'Simplicit y' (*su*) means literally 'raw silk'. It is the symbol of 1 attributeless' nature of Tao. The Uncarved Block is the symbol of the primal undifferentiated unity underlying the apparent complexity of the universe. *Ssŭ* (the 'self' element in the word translated selflessness) is the opposite of *kung*, 'public'. It means absence of personal ambition. For *kua-yü* 'fewness of desires', see Introduction, p. 89.

CHAPTER XX

Banish learning,[1] and there will be no more grieving.
Between *wei* and *o*
What after all is the difference?
Can it be compared to the difference between good and bad?[2]
The saying 'what others avoid I too must avoid'
How false and superficial it is!
All men, indeed, are wreathed in smiles,
As though feasting after the Great Sacrifice,
As though going up to the Spring Carnival.[3]
I alone am inert, like a child that has not yet given sign;[4]
Like an infant that has not yet smiled.
I droop and drift, as though I belonged nowhere.
All men have enough and to spare;
I alone seem to have lost everything.
Mine is indeed the mind of a very idiot,
So dull am I.
The world is full of people that shine;
I alone am dark.

[1] 'Learning' means in particular learning the '3300 rules of etiquette'. *Wei* and *o* were the formal and informal words for 'yes', each appropriate to certain occasions. For 'learning' in the sense of knowing which words are taboo at which Courts, see *Kuo Yü*, 15, fol. 3.

[2] Good and bad in the Taoist sense, i.e. like and unlike the Way. This leads up to the description of the great gulf that separates the Taoist from other men. This description is in the form of a generalized *jung* (see Ch. 15, above) and cannot be taken as in any sense a self-portrait of the author. The sense of the first six lines is very doubtful.

[3] See additional notes. I read *têng ch'un t'ai*.

[4] A child 'gives sign' by stretching its hand towards some object. This is an important omen concerning its future.

They look lively and self-assured;
I alone, depressed.
I seem unsettled[1] as the ocean;
Blown adrift, never brought to a stop.
All men can be put to some use;
I alone am intractable and boorish.
But wherein I most am different from men
Is that I prize no sustenance that comes not from the
    Mother's[2] breast.

Commentary

The saying 'What others avoid I too must avoid' refers
to keeping the same taboos, ritual avoidances, etc., as
people with whom one finds oneself in contact. Thus
Confucius (*Analects*, VII, 9), if he found himself eating
side by side with someone who was in mourning imposed
upon himself the same abstentions as were required of the
mourner. Conversely of course, it is ill-omened to weep
when others are rejoicing. But the Taoist, who is the anti-
thesis of other men, cannot obey these rules.

[1] For this sense of *tan*, see *Lü Shih Ch'un Ch'iu*, P'ien III, line 7.
[2] i.e. the Way's. The image may equally well be that of a child in
the womb, 'feeding on the mother'.

CHAPTER XXI

Such the scope of the All-pervading Power
That it alone can act through the Way.
For the Way is a thing impalpable, incommensurable.
Incommensurable, impalpable.
Yet latent in it are forms;[1]
Impalpable, incommensurable
Yet within it are entities.
Shadowy it is and dim;
Yet within it there is a force,
A force that though rarefied
Is none the less efficacious.
From the time of old till now
Its charge[2] has not departed
But cheers onward the many warriors.
How do I know that the many warriors are so?
Through this.[3]

---

[1] Thought-images, ideas.
[2] See additional notes.
[3] Through inward knowledge, intuition.

CHAPTER XXII

'To remain whole, be twisted!'
To become straight, let yourself be bent.
To become full, be hollow.
Be tattered, that you may be renewed.
Those that have little, may get more,
Those that have much, are but perplexed.
Therefore the Sage
Clasps the Primal Unity,
Testing by it everything under heaven.
He does not show himself; therefore he is seen everywhere.
He does not define himself, therefore he is distinct.
He does not boast of what he will do, therefore he succeeds.
He is not proud of his work, and therefore it endures.
He does not contend,
And for that very reason no one under heaven can contend with him.
So then we see that the ancient saying 'To remain whole, be twisted!' was no idle word; for true wholeness can only be achieved by return.[1]

[1] To the Way.

CHAPTER XXIII

To BE always talking is against nature. For the same reason a hurricane never lasts a whole morning, nor a rainstorm all day. Who is it that makes the wind and rain? It is Heaven-and-Earth.[1] And if even Heaven-and-Earth cannot blow or pour for long, how much less in his utterance should man? Truly, if one uses the Way[2] as one's instrument, the results will be like the Way; if one uses the 'power' as one's instrument, the results will be like the power. If one uses what is the reverse of the 'power', the results will be the reverse of the 'power'. For to those who have conformed themselves to the Way, the Way readily lends its power. To those who have conformed themselves to the power, the power readily lends more power. While to those who conform themselves to inefficacy, inefficacy readily lends its ineffectiveness. 'It is by not believing in people that you turn them into liars.'[3]

Commentary

Wind and rain are taken as the utterances of nature, parallel to speech in man. 'Talking' here refers to government by laws and proclamations. Tê, the power of Tao, also means 'getting' as opposed to 'loss', success as opposed to disaster. The author puns on these two senses, which were often expressed by the same character. For the silence of heaven, see *Analects*, XVII. 19; and for that of heaven and earth, see *Hsün Tzŭ*, P'ien 3, middle.

[1] Nature, as we should say.
[2] The text is here somewhat confused; but the general meaning is clear.   [3] See above, Ch. 17. If one uses disbelief as one's instrument of government, the result will be a nation of liars.

CHAPTER XXIV

'He who stands on tip-toe, does not stand firm;
He who takes the longest strides, does not walk the fastest.'
He who does his own looking sees little,
He who defines himself is not therefore distinct.
He who boasts of what he will do succeeds in nothing;
He who is proud of his work, achieves nothing that
    endures.
Of these, from the standpoint of the Way, it is said:
'Pass round superfluous dishes to those that have already
    had enough,
And no creature but will reject them in disgust.'
That is why he that possesses Tao does not linger.[1]

---

[1] Over the scene of his successes, thus calling attention to them.
Cf. Ch. 2.

CHAPTER XXV

There was something formless yet complete,
That existed before heaven and earth;
Without sound, without substance,
Dependent on nothing, unchanging,
All pervading, unfailing.
One may think of it as the mother of all things under
    heaven.
Its true name[1] we do not know;
'Way' is the by-name that we give it.
Were I forced to say to what class of things it belongs I
    should call it Great (*ta*).
Now *ta*[2] also means passing on,
And passing on means going Far Away,
And going far away means returning.[3]
Thus just as Tao[4] has 'this greatness' and as earth has it
and as heaven has it, so may the ruler also have it. Thus
'within the realm[2] there are four portions of greatness',
and one belongs to the king. The ways of men are con-
ditioned by those of earth. The ways of earth, by those
of heaven. The ways of heaven by those of Tao, and the
ways of Tao by the Self-so.[5]

---

[1] i.e. we do not know to what class of things it belongs.
[2] See textual notes.
[3] Returning to 'what was there at the Beginning'.
[4] Henceforward I shall use the Chinese word Tao instead of the
Way; to do so avoids many inconveniences.
[5] The 'unconditioned'; the 'what-is-so-of-itself'.

Tao Tê Ching

Commentary

The intention of this 'chain-argument' (a rhetorical form very commonly used by early Chinese writers) is to show that a line of connection may be traced between the ruler and Tao. This connection exists macrocosmically, in the line ruler, earth, heaven, Tao; but also microcosmically, in that by passing on and on through successive stages of his own consciousness back to the initial Unity he can arrive at the Way which controls the multiform apparent universe. The ecstasy called Far Away Wandering[1] is also known as the Far Away Passing On.[2]

The Realists insisted that there must be only one 'Greatness' in the realm—that of the State. I suspect that the clause 'There are four portions of greatness . . .' is adapted from a saying of the logicians. See Textual Notes.

---

[1] The subject of one of the *Ch'u Elegies*. These travels, these 'wanderings alone with Tao in the Great Wilderness' (*Chuang Tzŭ* XX. 2.) are not external journeys, but explorations of oneself, back to the 'Beginning of Things'.
[2] For example, in the *Li Sao*.

CHAPTER XXVI

As the heavy must be the foundation of the light,
So quietness is lord and master of activity.
Truly, 'A man of consequence[1] though he travels all day
Will not let himself be separated from his baggage-wagon,[2]
However magnificent the view, he sits quiet and dispassionate'.
How much less, then, must be the lord of ten thousand
    chariots
Allow himself to be lighter[3] than these he rules!
If he is light, the foundation is lost;
If he is active, the lord and master[4] is lost.

[1] Reading *Chün-tzŭ*, which has considerable ancient support; cf.
Ma Hsü-lun's *Lao Tzŭ Fu Ku*.

[2] Literally, 'his covered heavy', 'heavy' being the Chinese name for
carts as opposed to light travelling carriages. There is a play on the
two senses of 'heavy'. This is a patrician proverb, a maxim of the
chün-tzŭ, 'gentlemen'.

[3] i.e. more easily moved.

[4] i.e. Quietness, the magical passivity that is also called *wu-wei*.
There is a secondary meaning: 'His lordship is lost.'

CHAPTER XXVII

Perfect activity leaves no track behind it;
Perfect speech is like a jade-worker whose tool leaves no mark.
The perfect reckoner needs no counting-slips;[1]
The perfect door has neither bolt nor bar,
Yet cannot be opened.
The perfect knot needs neither rope nor twine,
Yet cannot be untied.
Therefore the Sage
Is all the time in the most perfect way helping men,
He certainly does not turn his back on men;
Is all the time in the most perfect way helping creatures,
He certainly does not turn his back on creatures.
This is called resorting to the Light.[2]
Truly, 'the perfect man is the teacher of the imperfect;
But the imperfect is the stock-in-trade[3] of the perfect man'.
He who does not respect his teacher,
He who does not take care of his stock-in-trade,
Much learning though he may possess, is far astray.
This[4] is the essential secret.

---

1 Slips of bamboo thrown into little bowls; forerunner of the abacus.
2 'Light' has been defined above as self-knowledge. 'This' means
the way in which the Sage saves the world, though apparently shunning
it. For 'resorting to' see additional notes.
3 Cf. *Chuang Tzŭ*, I. 4.
4 The power to influence mankind through Tao. The commonest
charge brought against Taoists was that of being merely interested in
self-perfection without regard for the welfare of the community as a
whole. The present chapter is devoted to rebutting that charge.

CHAPTER XXVIII

'He who knows the male, yet cleaves to what is female
Becomes like a ravine, receiving all things under heaven,'[1]
And being such a ravine
He knows all the time a power that he never calls upon in vain.
This is returning to the state of infancy.[2]
He who knows the white, yet cleaves to the black
Becomes the standard by which all things are tested;
And being such a standard
He has all the time a power that never errs,
He returns to the Limitless.
He who knows glory, yet cleaves to ignominy
Becomes like a valley that receives into it all things under
heaven,
And being such a valley
He has all the time a power that suffices;
He returns to the state of the Uncarved Block.
Now when a block is sawed up it is made into implements;[3]
But when the Sage uses it, it becomes Chief of all Ministers.
Truly, 'The greatest carver[4] does the least cutting'.

---

[1] Adapted from a Lao Tan saying. See *Chuang Tzŭ*, XXXIII. 5.
[2] Cf. Introduction, p. 55.
[3] Play on the double sense of this word which also means 'a sub-ordinate', 'an instrument of government'.
[4] Play on *chih* 'to cut', 'to carve', and *chih* 'to rule'. The secondary meaning is that the greatest ruler does the least chopping about.

CHAPTER XXIX

Those that would gain what is under heaven[1] by tamper-
ing with it—I have seen that they do not succeed. For
that which is under heaven is like a holy vessel,
dangerous to tamper with.
Those that tamper with it, harm it.
Those that grab at it, lose it.
For among the creatures of the world some go in front,
some follow;
Some blow hot when others would be blowing cold.
Some are feeling vigorous just when others are worn out.
Some are loading[2] just when others would be tilting out.
Therefore the Sage 'discards the absolute, the all-inclu-
sive,[3] the extreme'.

---

[1] i.e. empire.
[2] Read *tsai*.
[3] *Shê* means (1) 'spread out' (2) dissipated. It is the first meaning
which is appropriate here. The author is, however, certainly adapting
a maxim that was aimed against dissipation, luxury etc. cf. *Han Fei
Tzŭ*, P'ien 8, beginning.

179

CHAPTER XXX

a minister of quiet advising leader

He who by Tao purposes to help a ruler of men
Will oppose all conquest by force of arms;
For such things are wont to rebound.[1]
Where armies are, thorns and brambles grow.
The raising of a great host *(poverty)*
Is followed by a year of dearth.[2]
Therefore a good general effects his purpose and then
    stops; he does not take further advantage of his victory.
Fulfils his purpose and does not glory in what he has done;
Fulfils his purpose and does not boast of what he has done;
Fulfils his purpose, but takes no pride in what he has done;
Fulfils his purpose, but only as a step that could not be
    avoided.[3]
Fulfils his purpose, but without violence;
For what has a time of vigour also has a time of decay.
This[4] is against Tao,
And what is against Tao will soon perish.

[1] Lit. 'To be reversed'. He who overcomes by violence will himself
be overcome by violence.

[2] This does not only refer to direct destruction, but also to the curse
that war brings upon herds and crops by its intrinsic 'balefulness'.

[3] For the construction compare *Chuang Tzŭ* XXIII. 6: 'To move
only when movement cannot be avoided, that is the true power.' This
principle of *pu tê i* 'action as a last resort' was preached by the 4th
century Quietist Shên Tao, and pervades *Chuang Tzŭ*.

[4] Violence.

CHAPTER XXXI

FINE[1] WEAPONS are none the less ill-omened things. That is why, among people of good birth,[2] in peace the left-hand side[3] is the place of honour, but in war this is reversed and the right-hand side is the place of honour. The Quietist,[4] even when he conquers, does not regard weapons as lovely things. For to think them lovely means to delight in them, and to delight in them means to delight in the slaughter of men. And he who delights in the slaughter of men will never get what he looks for out of those that dwell under heaven. A host that has slain men is received with grief and mourning; he that has conquered in battle is[5] received with rites of mourning.

Commentary

In this chapter, as has been generally recognized, a considerable amount of commentary has become inextricably confused with the text. Now upon this chapter Wang Pi[6] makes no comments. The natural inference, as

1 *Chia* also means 'auspicious', e.g. *chia jih*, 'a lucky day'. I see no reason to tamper with the text.

2 Of good birth, and consequently of good manners.

3 See additional notes.

4 For this expression cf. *Han Fei Tzǔ*, P'ien 51, near end, and *Chuang Tzǔ*, X, end.

5 Whether such a custom actually existed we do not know; but we learn from *Huai-nan Tzǔ* (15, end) that the general, having received his marching orders, cuts his nails (as was done by mourners before a funeral), dresses in mourning garb, and leaves the city by a 'gate of ill-omen' constructed for the purpose.

6 226-249 A.D. The earliest commentator on the *Tao Tê Ching* whose work survives.

181

the Japanese scholar Tojo Hiroshi has pointed out,[1] is that the text as we have it is an amalgamation of the original with the lost Wang Pi commentary. Several attempts[2] have been made to separate this intrusive commentary from the text. My reconstruction comes fairly close to that of Ma Hsü-lun (1924).[3]

[1] In his *Roshi Ochu Hyoshi*, 1814.
[2] e.g. by T'ao Fang-chi, Li Tz'ŭ-ming and Ma Hsü-lun.
[3] It should however be noted, in connection with the above line of argument, that there is also no Wang Pi commentary on Ch. 66.

CHAPTER XXXII

Tao is eternal, but has no fame (name);[1]
The Uncarved Block,[2] though seemingly of small account,
Is greater than anything that is under heaven.[3]
If kings and barons would but possess themselves of it,
The ten thousand creatures would flock to do them homage;
Heaven-and-earth would conspire
To send Sweet Dew,[4]
Without law or compulsion, men would dwell in harmony.
Once the block is carved,[5] there will be names,[6]
And so soon as there are names
Know that it is time to stop.
Only by knowing when it is time to stop can danger be avoided.
To Tao[7] all under heaven will come
As streams and torrents flow into a great river or sea.

[1] See textual notes.
[2] See Ch. 28.
[3] Literally 'under Heaven no one dares regard it as an inferior'.
[4] 'Sweet Dew tastes like barley-sugar or honey; it falls only when a kingdom is at complete peace.' *Lun Hêng*, XIX. 2. See also *Kuan Tzŭ*, P'ien 20, fol. 16, and *Lü Shih Ch'un Ch'iu*, 115, end.
[5] Secondary meaning 'Once there is government'.
[6] Categories, distinctions. Things depending on contrast with something else; as opposed to Tao, which 'is so of itself'.
[7] i.e. to the possessor of Tao. The last two lines resume the thought of lines 4 and 5.

CHAPTER XXXIII

To understand others is to have knowledge;
To understand oneself is to be illumined.
To conquer others needs strength;
To conquer oneself is harder still.
To be content with what one has is to be rich.
He that works through[1] violence may get his way;
But only what stays[2] in its place
Can endure.
When one dies one is not lost;[3] there is no other longevity.

Commentary

Shou longevity means, strictly speaking, potential longevity, 'staying-power', what we should call having a good constitution, and is a quality that may be possessed by the young as well as the old. One branch of the 'life-nurturing' school sought it by means of diet, hygiene, drugs, etc. For the Taoist view of death see Introduction, p. 54.

[1] The word hsing implies movement as well as action.
[2] As, for example, mountains.
[3] One's left arm may become a cock; one's right arm a bow; one's buttocks wheels (Chuang Tzŭ VI. 6). In any case, no part of one will be lost.

CHAPTER XXXIV

Great Tao is like a boat that drifts;
It can go this way; it can go that.
The ten thousand creatures owe their existence to it and it does
    not disown them;
Yet having produced them, it does not take possession of them.[1]
Tao, though it covers the ten thousand things like a garment,
Makes no claim to be master over them,
And asks for nothing from them.
Therefore it may be called the Lowly:
The ten thousand creatures obey it,
Though they know not that they have a master;
Therefore it is called the Great.
So too the Sage just because he never at any time makes a show
of greatness in fact achieves greatness.

[1] Cf. Chapter 2, where similar words are used of the Sage, who is
identified with Tao. For the reading, see textual notes.

CHAPTER XXXV

He who holding the Great Form goes about his work in
    the empire
Can go about his work, yet do no harm.
All is peace, quietness and security.
Sound of music, smell of good dishes
Will make the passing stranger pause.
How different the words that Tao gives forth!
So thin, so flavourless!
If one looks for Tao, there is nothing solid to see;
If one listens for it, there is nothing loud enough to hear.
Yet if one uses it, it is inexhaustible.

Commentary

The Great Form is the form that is formless, i.e. Tao.
Strictly speaking the word means a mental image as
opposed to concrete reality.

See introduction p. 61, *hsiang*.

CHAPTER XXXVI

What is in the end to be shrunk
Must first be stretched.
Whatever is to be weakened
Must begin by being made strong.
What is to be overthrown
Must begin by being set up.
He who would be a taker
Must begin as a giver.
This is called 'dimming' one's light.[1]
It is thus that the soft overcomes the hard
And the weak, the strong.
'It is best to leave the fish down in his pool;
Best to leave the State's sharpest weapons where none can
    see them.'

Commentary

The Sage must 'stoop to conquer', must make himself
small in order to be great, must be cast down before he
can be exalted. He must remain like the fish at the bottom of the pool. The last two lines are a maxim of common statecraft, here applied in a metaphorical way: the
'sharp weapons' symbolize the Taoist sage who is a kind
of secret armament on whom the safety of the state depends. The fish symbolizes armour because both have
'scales'. Compare the I Chou Shu 52, where it is said that
on the tenth day of spring the fish come up above the ice.
If they fail to do so, this is a sign that armour is being secret-
ed in the houses of private people with a view to rebellion.

1 Wei means (1) 'obscure because so small', (2) 'obscure because so
dark'. It is etymologically connected with mei 'dark'.

187

CHAPTER XXXVII

Tao never does;
Yet through it all things are done.
If the barons and kings would but possess themselves of it,
The ten thousand creatures would at once be transformed.
And if having been transformed they should desire to act,
We must restrain them by the blankness[1] of the Unnamed.
The blankness of the Unnamed
Brings dispassion;
To be dispassionate is to be still.
And so,[2] of itself, the whole empire will be at rest.

---

[1] Literally, 'the uncarven-wood-quality'.
[2] If the Sage is 'still'.

CHAPTER XXXVIII

The man of highest 'power' does not reveal himself as a
    possessor of 'power';
Therefore he keeps his 'power'.
The man of inferior 'power' cannot rid it of the appear-
    ance of 'power';
Therefore he is in truth without 'power'.
The man of highest 'power' neither acts[1] nor is there any
    who so regards him;[2]
The man of inferior 'power' both acts and is so regarded.[3]
The man of highest humanity, though he acts, is not so
    regarded;
Whereas a man of even the highest morality both acts and
    is so regarded.
While even he who is best versed in ritual not merely
    acts, but if people fail to respond
Then he will pull up his sleeves and advance upon them.
That is why it is said:[4] 'After Tao was lost, then came the
    "power";
After the "power" was lost, then came human kindness.
After human kindness was lost, then came morality,
After morality was lost, then came ritual.
Now ritual is the mere husk[5] of loyalty and promise-
    keeping

1 Does not act separately and particularly, but only applies the
'power' in a general way.
2 Regards him as a possessor of power. Compare *Kuan Tzŭ*, P'ien 5,
paragraph 2.   3 i.e. is regarded as a possessor of *tê*.
4 The same saying is quoted by *Chuang Tzŭ*, XXII. 1.
5 Or 'attenuated form'; but it balances *hua* ('flower', as opposed to
fruit) and it is better to indicate the vegetable metaphor.

And is indeed the first step towards brawling.'
Foreknowledge[1] may be the 'flower of doctrine',
But it is the beginning of folly.
Therefore the full-grown man[2] takes his stand upon the
    solid substance and not upon the mere husk,
Upon the fruit and not upon the flower.
Truly, 'he rejects that and takes this'.

(The repeated use of nouns as verbs, not possible in English to the same extent as in Chinese, makes anything but a clumsy paraphrase of the first ten lines of the chapter impossible.)

---

[1] See additional notes.   [2] Full-grown in Tao.

CHAPTER XXXIX

As for the things that from of old have understood the Whole—
The sky through such understanding remains limpid,
Earth remains steady,
The spirits keep their holiness,[1]
The abyss is replenished,
The ten thousand creatures bear their kind,
Barons and princes direct[2] their people.
It is the Whole that causes it.
Were it not so limpid, the sky would soon get torn,
Were it not for its steadiness, the earth would soon tip over,
Were it not for their holiness, the spirits would soon wither
   away.
Were it not for this replenishment, the abyss would soon go dry,
Were it not that the ten thousand creatures can bear their kind,
They would soon become extinct.
Were the barons and princes no longer directors of their people
   and for that reason honoured and exalted, they would soon
   be overthrown.
Truly 'the humble is the stem upon which the mighty grows,
The low is the foundation upon which the high is laid.'
That is why barons and princes refer to themselves as 'The
Orphan', 'The Needy', 'The Ill-provided'. Is this not indeed a
case of might rooting itself upon humility?[3]

[1] Their *ling*, which is to spirits (or objects and animals 'possessed' by spirits)
what *tê* is to man. It is cognate to words meaning life, name, command, etc.

[2] See additional notes.   [3] From 'Truly' to 'humility' is quoted with
slight variants by the *Chan Kuo Ts'ê* (IV. 14 recto) as a saying of Lao Tzŭ. It
is probable that we have here an actual quotation of the *Tao Tê Ching*. For
the date of the *Chan Kuo Ts'ê*, see Appendix VI.

191

True indeed are the sayings:
'Enumerate the parts of a carriage, and you still have not explained what a carriage' is, and 'They[1] did not want themselves to tinkle like jade-bells, while others resounded like stone-chimes'.

Commentary

'Have understood the Whole'; literally 'Have got the Whole'. But the parallel passage in *Chuang Tzŭ* (XXV. 10) uses the expression 'getting a horse' in the sense of realizing what a horse is, as opposed to knowing what its parts (ears, body, tail, etc.) are. 'Get' therefore here means 'get the idea of'. Compare our colloquial expression 'Do you get me?' Of the two sayings at the end of the chapter, the first illustrates the theme of 'understanding the Whole' with which the chapter opens; the second recapitulates the latter part of the chapter, which deals with the reluctance of the wise ruler to put himself 'above' his subjects and so spoil the unity of empire.

In line 8, the words 'It is the Whole' are accidentally omitted in the Wang Pi text.

CHAPTER XL

In Tao the only motion is returning;[2]
The only useful quality, weakness.
For though all creatures under heaven are the products of Being,
Being itself is the product of Not-being.

---

[1] The Sages of old. [2] Compare Ch. XXV, line 12.

CHAPTER XLI

When the man of highest capacities hears Tao
He does his best to put it into practice.
When the man of middling capacity hears Tao
He is in two minds about it.
When the man of low capacity hears Tao
He laughs loudly at it.
If he did not laugh, it would not be worth the name of Tao.
Therefore the proverb has it:
'The way[1] out into the light often looks dark,
The way that goes ahead often looks as if it went back.'
The way that is least hilly often looks as if it went up and down,
The 'power' that is really loftiest looks like an abyss,
What is sheerest white looks blurred.
The 'power' that is most sufficing looks inadequate,
The 'power' that stands firmest looks flimsy.[2]
What is in its natural, pure state looks faded;[2]
The largest square has no corners,
The greatest vessel takes the longest to finish,[3]
Great music has the faintest[4] notes,
The Great Form[5] is without shape.
For Tao is hidden and nameless.
Yet Tao alone supports[6] all things and brings them to fulfilment.

---

[1] Tao.
[2] See additional notes.
[3] Metaphorical meaning, 'The greatest capacities develop latest'.
[4] 'Most rarefied.' Cf. Ch. 14.
[5] Cf. Ch. 35.
[6] A commercial metaphor. Literally 'backs financially'.

Tao Tê Ching

Commentary

'The largest vessel. . . .' When the great Han dynasty general Ma Yüan[1] was young, he was worried by the fact that he could not understand or get any pleasure from the *Book of Odes*, but preferred hunting. 'I am sure', his brother told him, 'you have "high capacities" that will "develop late". A good craftsman does not show his work while it is still in the rough. The best thing you can do for the present is to go off and have as much fun as you can.'

---

[1] *Hou Han Shu*, Ch. XXIV, fol. 1.

CHAPTER XLII

TAO GAVE birth to the One; the One gave birth successively to two things, three things, up to ten thousand.[1] These ten thousand creatures cannot turn their backs to the shade without having the sun on their bellies,[2] and it is on this blending of the breaths[3] that their harmony[4] depends. To be orphaned, needy, ill-provided is what men most hate; yet princes and dukes style themselves so. Truly, 'things are often increased by seeking to diminish them and diminished by seeking to increase them.' The maxims that others use in their teaching I too will use in mine. Show me a man of violence that came to a good end,[5] and I will take him for my teacher.

Commentary

To be a prince is a 'sunny' as opposed to a 'shady' thing. But a prince does not feel properly 'harmonized' unless he also has 'the shade at his back', which he obtains by humbling himself.

A proverb[6] says: 'The man of violence never yet came to a good end; nor did he that delights in victory fail to meet his match.' Another proverb[7] says: 'The best doctor

[1] i.e. everything.

[2] Which symbolizes the fact that they are themselves a mixture of light and dark, hard and soft, water and fire, etc.

[3] The warm 'breath' of the sun and the cold 'breath' of the shade. Hence 'breath' comes to mean a 'state of the atmosphere' in a wider sense.

[4] Or 'balance', as we should say.   [5] See textual notes.

[6] See additional notes.   [7] See *Hou Han Shu*, XXX. fol. 3.

cannot save one whose life-span has run out; nor can the man of violence strive with Heaven.' It is possible that *Ch'iang-liang*, 'man of violence', is in reality the name of a mythological figure, a sort of Titan who warred unsuccessfully against Heaven. *Ch'iang* means 'violent'; but *liang* means 'rafter', and though the two together are said to mean 'man of violence', no proof is adduced; and I suspect that this Titan was called 'Rafter' because his image was carved on the ends of rafters. This theory is borne out by a passage in *Chuang Tzŭ* (VI. 9) which speaks of a strong man called Chü-liang, 'holder of the rafters' who like Samson 'lost his strength'. In order to conform to a quotation by *Huai-nan Tzŭ*, many modern editors have tampered with the text at the beginning of the chapter.

CHAPTER XLIII

What is of all things most yielding[1]
Can overwhelm that which is of all things most hard.[2]
Being substanceless it can enter even where there is no space;
That is how I know the value of action that is actionless.
But that there can be teaching without words,
Value in action that is actionless,
Few indeed can understand.

CHAPTER XLIV

Fame or one's own self, which matters to one most?
One's own self or things bought, which should count most?
In the getting or the losing, which is worse?[3]
Hence he who grudges expense pays dearest in the end;
He who has hoarded most will suffer the heaviest loss.[4]
Be content with what you have and are, and no one can despoil
    you;
Who stops in time nothing can harm.
He is forever safe and secure.

    [1] Water.   [2] Rock.
    [3] i.e. which is better, to get fame and wealth but injure oneself, or to lack fame and wealth and save oneself?
    [4] He drives people to such exasperation that they attack him and help themselves. For *ai* in the sense 'grudge' compare *I Chou Shu* 54, 'He who is stingy about rewards and gifts is called *ai*'. The primary meaning of *ai* is 'to want to keep to oneself'. Hence the commoner meaning 'to love', which would here be out of place.

CHAPTER XLV

What is most perfect seems to have something missing;
Yet its use is unimpaired.[1]
What is most full seems empty;
Yet its use will never fail.[2]
What is most straight seems crooked;
The greatest skill seems like clumsiness,
The greatest eloquence like stuttering.[3]
Movement overcomes cold;
But staying still overcomes heat.
So he[4] by his limpid calm
Puts right everything under heaven.

[1] Metaphor of a pot or vessel; applied to Tao.
[2] It can be drawn upon indefinitely.
[3] Compare *Analects* IV, 24; and the stuttering of Moses (*Encyclopædia of Islam*, under Musa).   [4] The Sage.

CHAPTER XLVI

When there is Tao in the empire
The galloping[1] steeds *(war horse)* are turned back to fertilize the
  ground by their droppings.
When there is not Tao in the empire *(ancestors are buried here)*
War horses will be reared even on the sacred mounds[2]
  below the city walls.
No lure[3] is greater than to possess what others want,
No disaster greater than not to be content with what one
  has,
No presage of evil greater than that men should be want-
  ing to get more.
Truly: 'He who has once known the contentment that
  comes simply through being content, will never again
  be otherwise than contented'.

---

[1] i.e. carriage-horses, used not for war but for travelling. Every one
will be contented where he is.

[2] See additional notes. They are reared, of course, as a preparation
for offensive war, i.e. for 'getting more'.

[3] i.e. incitement to evil doers. See additional notes.

CHAPTER XLVII

Without leaving his door
He knows everything under heaven.
Without looking out of his window
He knows all the ways of heaven.
For the further one travels[1]
The less one knows.
Therefore the Sage arrives without going,
Sees all[2] without looking,
Does nothing, yet achieves everything.

[1] Away from Tao; away from the Unity into the Multiplicity.
[2] Read *ming* 'illumined', not *ming* 'name'. The two characters are constantly interchanged in old texts.

CHAPTER XLVIII

Learning consists in adding to one's stock day by day;
The practice of Tao consists in 'subtracting day by day,
Subtracting and yet again subtracting
Till one has reached inactivity.
But by this very inactivity
Everything can be activated.'[1]
Those who of old won the adherence of all who live under
    heaven
All did so by not interfering.
Had they interfered,
They would never have won this adherence.

---

[1] Compare *Chuang Tzŭ* XXII. 1.

CHAPTER XLIX

The Sage has no heart[1] of his own;
He uses the heart of the people as his heart.
Of the good man I[2] approve,
But of the bad I also approve,
And thus he gets goodness.
The truthful man I believe, but the liar I also believe,
And thus he gets truthfulness.[3]
The Sage, in his dealings with the world, seems like one
    dazed with fright;[4]
For the world's sake he dulls his wits.
The Hundred Families all the time strain their eyes and
    ears,[5]
The Sage all the time sees and hears no more than an in-
fant sees and hears.

---

[1] Makes no judgments of his own.
[2] i.e. the Sage.
[3] Cf. Ch. 17 and 23.
[4] Read 'heart' beside 'leaf'.
[5] This line is accidentally omitted by the Wang Pi text.

CHAPTER L

HE WHO aims at life achieves death. If the 'companions of life'[1] are thirteen, so likewise are the 'companions of death' thirteen. How is it that the 'death-spots'[2] in man's life and activity are also thirteen? It is because men feed life too grossly. It is said that he who has a true hold on life, when he walks on land[3] does not meet tigers or wild buffaloes; in battle he is not touched by weapons of war. Indeed, a buffalo that attacked him would find nothing for its horns to butt, a tiger would find nothing for its claws to tear, a weapon would find no place for its point to enter in.[4] And why? Because such men have no 'death-spot' in them.

Commentary

In military language 'he who *ch'u ssŭ*[5] "goes out prepared to die" comes back alive and victorious'. Conversely, he who 'goes for' (aims at) life, achieves death. This is here adapted as an attack on the Hedonists, who maintained that the aim of life consists in giving satis-

1 The four limbs and nine apertures that constitute the human apparatus.
2 A military expression.
3 One would expect this to balance a clause about what happens when he is on the water.
4 Compare *Chuang Tzŭ* XVII. 1, end.
5 Cf. *Han Fei Tzŭ* P'ien 50: How can soldiers be expected to 'go out prepared to die', when at home admiration is accorded to those whose consciences (*i*) forbid them to enter endangered towns, dwell in camps, or in fact give one hair of their bodies, even if it would benefit the whole world?

Tao Tê Ching

faction to every constituent part of the human apparatus. But excessive 'feeding of life', says our author, defeats its own end, creating 'death-spots' (as I have said, this too is a military term). Ordinary people by 'fostering life' convert their thirteen constituent parts, which might be 'companions of life', into 'companions of death'.

We attribute the fact that some people do not meet tigers or get killed in battle to a thing we call 'chance'. The Taoist attributed such immunity to qualities in the 'lucky' person himself. Their view has perhaps as much to be said for it as ours. All efforts to make *shih yu san* mean anything but 'thirteen' do violence both to idiom and sense.

CHAPTER LI

Tao gave them birth;
The 'power' of Tao reared them,
Shaped them according to their kinds,
Perfected them, giving to each its strength.[1]
Therefore of the ten thousand things[2] there is not one that
does not worship Tao and do homage to its 'power'. No
mandate ever went forth that accorded to Tao the right to
be worshipped, nor to its 'power' the right to receive
homage.
It was always and of itself so.
Therefore as Tao bore them and the 'power' of Tao reared
them, made them grow, fostered them, harboured them,
brewed[3] for them, so you[4] must
'Rear them, but not lay claim to them,
Control them, but never lean upon them,
Be chief among them, but not manage them.
This is called the mysterious power.'[5]

[1] Its 'strong point', inborn capacity.
[2] Excepting Man?
[3] The word means a 'decoction', whether nutritive, medicinal or
(as always in modern Chinese) poisonous.
[4] The Sage.
[5] Cf. Chapter 10.

CHAPTER LII

That which was the beginning of all things under heaven
We may speak of as the 'mother' of all things.
He who apprehends the mother[1]
Thereby knows the sons.[2]
And he who has known the sons
Will hold all the tighter to the mother,
And to the end of his days suffer no harm:
'Block the passages, shut the doors,
And till the end your strength shall not fail.
Open up the passages, increase your doings,
And till your last day no help shall come to you.'
As good sight means seeing what is very small
So strength means holding on to what is weak.[3]
He who having used the outer-light[4] can return to the
    inner-light
Is thereby preserved from all harm.
This is called resorting to the always-so.

[1] Tao, the One, the Whole.
[2] The Many, the universe.
[3] i.e. Tao.
[4] This corresponds to 'knowing the sons'. *Ming* ('inner light') is
self-knowledge.

CHAPTER LIII

HE WHO has the least scrap[1] of sense, once he has got
started on the great highway has nothing to fear so long as
he avoids turnings. For great highways are safe and easy.
But men love by-paths.[2]
So long as the Court is in order
They are content to let their fields run to weed
And their granaries stand empty.
They wear patterns and embroideries,
Carry sharp swords, glut themselves with drink and food,
 have more possessions than they can use.
These are the riotous ways of brigandage;[3] they are not the
 Highway.

---

[1] See additional notes.

[2] All this is of course metaphorical. The highway is Tao; the by-
paths, the Confucian virtues. 'Loving by-paths' implies also neglecting
the essential and pursuing the secondary.

[3] Compare the riotous ways of the Robber Chê in *Chuang Tzŭ*.

CHAPTER LIV

What Tao[1] plants cannot be plucked,
What Tao clasps, cannot slip.
By its virtue alone can one generation after another carry on the
ancestral sacrifice.[2]
Apply it to yourself and by its power you will be freed from dross.
Apply it to your household and your household shall thereby
have abundance.
Apply it to the village, and the village will be made secure.
Apply it to the kingdom, and the kingdom shall thereby be
made to flourish.
Apply it to an empire, and the empire shall thereby be extended.
Therefore just as through[3] oneself one may contemplate Oneself,
So through the household one may contemplate the Household,[4]
And through the village, one may contemplate the Village,
And through the kingdom, one may contemplate the Kingdom,
And through the empire, one may contemplate the Empire.
How do I know that the empire is so?
By this.[5]

---

[1] Literally 'what is well planted', i.e. planted by Tao.

[2] The 'power' of the ancestor's Tao carries the family on.

[3] By delving back through the successive stages of one's own conscious one gets back to the Unity of the Whole which is one's Tao. Cf. the *Maitri Upanishad* (Hume, p. 435) 'having seen the Self through oneself one becomes selfless'.

[4] i.e. the Tao of the household. When one has had vision of the Tao (underlying essence) of a thing, one can control it. This catena (self-household-village, etc.) is found in every branch of Chinese philosophy, applied in a variety of ways. It originated I think with the Yang Chu theory that to perfect a family one must perfect the individual members of it, to perfect a village one must perfect each several family, etc.   [5] What is inside me.

CHAPTER LV

The impunity of things fraught with the 'power'
May be likened to that of an infant.
Poisonous insects do not sting it,
Nor fierce beasts seize it,
Nor clawing birds maul it.
Its bones are soft, its sinews weak; but its grip is strong.
Not yet to have known the union of male and female, but to be
    completely formed,
Means that the vital force is at its height;
To be able to scream all day without getting hoarse
Means that harmony[1] is at its perfection.
To understand such harmony[2] is to understand the always-so.
To understand the always-so is to be illumined.
But to fill life to the brim is to invite omens.[3]
If the heart makes calls upon the life-breath,[4] rigidity follows.
Whatever has a time of vigour also has a time of decay.
Such[5] things are against Tao,
And whatever is against Tao is soon destroyed.

[1] Of hot and cold, soft and hard, etc. For the state of infancy as a
Taoist ideal, see Introduction, p. 55

[2] Compare *Analects*, I. 12.

[3] Here, as in the Short Preface to the *Book of History* (Legge, p. 6)
and *Shih Chi*, Ch. III, fol. 6, *hsiang* means a bad omen. It originally
meant a portent of any kind, whether good or bad. In current Chinese
it is, of course, only used in the favourable sense.

[4] The emotions were thought by the Chinese to make call upon and
use up the original supply of breath which was allotted to a man at
birth and constituted his life-spirit.

[5] Filling to the brim, calling upon the life-breath, having a time of
'vigour'. Cf. Ch. 30.

CHAPTER LVI

Those who know do not speak;
Those who speak do not know.
Block the passages,
Shut the doors,
Let all sharpness be blunted,
All tangles untied,
All glare tempered.
All dust smoothed.[1]
This is called the mysterious levelling.[2]
He who has achieved it cannot either be drawn into
    friendship or repelled,
Cannot be benefited, cannot be harmed,
Cannot either be raised or humbled,
And for that very reason is highest of all creatures under
    heaven.

---

[1] Cf. Ch. 4.
[2] In which there is a general perception not effected through particular senses. See *Lieh Tzǔ*, II. 3. 'Henceforward my eyes were one with my ears, my ears with my nose, my nose with my mouth. . . .'

CHAPTER LVII

'Kingdoms can only be governed if rules are kept;
Battles can only be won if rules are broken.'[1]
But the adherence of all under heaven can only be won by
letting-alone.
How do I know that it is so?
By this.[2]
The more prohibitions there are, the more ritual avoidances,
The poorer the people will be.
The more 'sharp weapons'[3] there are,
The more benighted will the whole land grow.
The more cunning craftsmen there are,
The more pernicious contrivances[4] will be invented.
The more laws are promulgated,
The more thieves and bandits there will be.
Therefore a sage has said:
So long as I 'do nothing' the people will of themselves be trans-
formed.
So long as I love quietude, the people will of themselves go
straight.
So long as I act only by inactivity the people will of themselves
become prosperous.
So long as I have no wants the people will of themselves return
to the 'state of the Uncarved Block'.

1 A military maxim, to the pattern of which the author proceeds to fit his
Taoist formula. Cf. Lionel Giles, *Sun Tzŭ* pp. 34, 35. *Ch'i* means unex-
pected manœuvres. *Chêng* 'rules kept' is not here used in its technical military sense of 'open attack'.
2 See Ch. 12. Through what I have found inside myself, 'in the belly';
through the light of my inner vision.   3 i.e. clever people.
4 Cf. the story in *Chuang Tzŭ* (XII. 11) about the man in whom the idea of
a simple labour-saving contrivance inspired feelings similar to those aroused
in Wordsworth by the sight of a railway train.

CHAPTER LVIII

When the ruler looks depressed[1] the people will be happy
    and satisfied;
When the ruler looks lively and self-assured[2] the people
    will be carping and discontented.
'It is upon bad fortune that good fortune leans, upon good
    fortune that bad fortune rests.'[3]
But though few know it, there is a bourn where there is
    neither right nor wrong;[4]
In a realm· where every straight is doubled by a crooked,
    and every good by an ill, surely mankind has gone
    long enough astray?
Therefore the Sage
Squares without cutting,
Shapes the corners without lopping,
Straightens without stretching,
Gives forth light without shining.[5]

1 As the Taoist is described as doing in Ch. 20.
2 Like the people of the world in Ch. 20.
3 Such are the maxims that pass as wisdom. The author is here
manifestly satirizing a passage in the *Lü Shih Ch'un Ch'iu* (P'ien 29,
beginning): 'It is upon bad fortune that good fortune leans, upon good
fortune that bad fortune rests. The Sage alone perceives this. How
should ordinary men reach such a bourn (of wisdom)?' To the Taoist
the real 'bourn of wisdom' lies far beyond the world of contraries
and antinomies.
4 *Hsieh*, omitted by some versions of the Wang Pi text, should be
retained.
5 Through Tao he reaches his *ends* without use of *means*. To translate
'shines without dazzling' is to misunderstand the whole sequence.
The Confucians as their 'means' use the virtues of 'squareness', i.e.
rectitude, and 'angularity' i.e. incorruptibility.

CHAPTER LIX

You cannot rule men nor serve heaven unless you have laid up a
  store;
This 'laying up a store' means quickly absorbing,[1]
And 'quickly absorbing' means doubling one's garnered 'power'.
Double your garnered power and it acquires a strength that
  nothing can overcome.
If there is nothing it cannot overcome, it knows no bounds,
And only what knows no bounds
Is huge enough to keep a whole kingdom in its grasp.
But only he who having the kingdom goes to the Mother
Can keep it long.
This[2] is called the art of making the roots strike deep by fencing
the trunk, of making life long by fixed staring.

Commentary

There is a common saying, which takes a variety of
different forms, 'With but one year's store, a land is a
land no more'. In order that the food of the living and of
the dead[3] may be assured in case of a failure of the crops
or an invasion, part of last year's grain must be retained in
the barns as a basis for the new store. This 'laying of the
new upon the old' is here used as a symbol for the rein-
forcing of one's stock of vital-energy (ch'i, 'breath') by
Quietist practices. Compare Mencius's famous hao-jan
chih ch'i 'welling breath' which issuing from such a

1 See textual notes.
2 i.e. going to Tao the Mother.
3 i.e. sacrifices to the Ancestors (Heaven).

'garnered store' as our author here describes was so great and strong 'that it would fill heaven, earth and all that is in between'. There is little reason to doubt that 'fixed staring' was used by the Taoists, as it was by Indians and by Byzantine Quietists, as a method of trance induction. Non-Taoists used the phrase without understanding it, imagining apparently that it was synonymous with *ch'ang-shêng*, 'long life'. Cf. *Hsün Tzŭ* 4, middle, and *Lü Shih Ch'un Ch'iu* 3, fol. 2.

CHAPTER LX

RULING A large kingdom is indeed like cooking small fish.[1] They who by Tao ruled all that is under heaven did not let an evil spirit[2] within them display its powers. Nay, it was not only that the evil spirit did not display its powers; neither was the Sage's good spirit[3] used to the hurt of other men. Nor was it only that his good spirit was not used to harm other men, the Sage himself was thus saved from harm.[4] And so, each being saved from harm, their 'powers' could converge towards a common end.

Commentary

A number of parallel passages, which the author quite certainly had in mind, make it evident that both *kuei* and *shên* are here used in a subjective sense: 'The enlightened (i.e. Realist) monarch in the carrying out of his institutes is a god (*t'ien*); in his use of men he is a demon (*kuei*).[5] He is a god, in that he cannot be gainsaid; a demon, in that he is subject to no restraint.'[6] 'The Sages of old did not damage their souls (*shên*)' by evil passions.[7] Another parallel passage, containing both a reference to *kuei* and the

[1] The less one handles them the better. [2] *Kuei.* [3] *Shên.*
[4] Omit *jên*, which has crept in under the influence of Han Fei Tzŭ who is, I think, simply adapting a traditional text to his own purposes. (P'ien 20, fol. 9.)
[5] A *kuei* is not of course necessarily bad. It is simply the spirit of a commoner as opposed to that of a dweller in heaven (*t'ien*) i.e. a Former King. But 'possession' by a *kuei* was always evil.
[6] *Han Fei Tzŭ*, 48. 1. [7] *Lü Shih Ch'un Ch'iu*, 119.

curious sequence of a statement followed by 'Nay, it was not so . . .' was certainly also in the author's mind: 'If with the whole essence of your being you ponder on a question, the *kuei* will give you the answer. Nay, it is not that the *kuei* answer you, it is simply that you have pondered with the whole essence of your being.'[1]

The general meaning is that if the ruler follows the Realist's advice and is a 'demon' in his dealings with the people, he will do as much harm to his own soul as to them.

---

[1] *Lü Shih Ch'un Ch'iu*, 147.

CHAPTER LXI

A LARGE kingdom must be like the low ground towards which all streams flow down. It must be a point towards which all things under heaven converge. Its part must be that of the female in its dealings with all things under heaven. The female by quiescence conquers the male; by quiescence gets underneath.[1] If a large kingdom can in the same way succeed in getting underneath a small kingdom then it will win the adherence of the small kingdom; and it is because small kingdoms are by nature in this way underneath large kingdoms that they win the adherence of large kingdoms. The one must get underneath in order to do it; the other is underneath and therefore does it. What large countries really need is more inhabitants; and what small countries need is some place where their surplus inhabitants can go and get employment. Thus[2] each gets what it needs. That is why I say the large kingdom must 'get underneath'.

[1] Literally 'becomes underneath', i.e. induces the male to mount her.
[2] i.e. if the large kingdom 'gets underneath'. It is assumed that the population of the large kingdom will be relatively sparse; that of the small kingdom relatively dense.

CHAPTER LXII

Tao in the Universe is like the south-west corner[1] in the
    house.
It is the treasure of the good man,
The support of the bad.
There is a traffic in speakers of fine words;
Persons of grave demeanour are accepted as gifts;
Even the bad let slip no opportunity to acquire them.
Therefore[2] on the day of an Emperor's enthronement
Or at the installation of the three officers of State
Rather than send a team of four horses, preceded by a disc
    of jade,
Better were it, as can be done without moving from one's
    seat, to send this Tao.
For what did the ancients say of this Tao, how did they
prize it? Did they not say of those that have it 'Pursuing,
they shall catch; pursued, they shall escape?' They thought
it, indeed, most precious of all things under heaven.

Commentary

The 'speakers of fine words' and 'persons of grave demeanour' were the itinerant sophists and sages who at
that time went round from capital to capital, selling their
services to the ruler who offered them the highest induce-
ments.

[1] Where family worship was carried on; the pivotal point round
which the household centred.
[2] i.e. if things other than presents in kind are not only accepted as
gifts, but even purchased at high price.

CHAPTER LXIII

It acts without action, does without doing, finds flavour in
    what is flavourless,[1]
Can make the small great and the few many,
'Requites injuries with good deeds,
Deals with the hard while it is still easy,
With the great while it is still small.'[2]
In the governance of empire everything difficult must be
    dealt with while it is still easy,
Everything great must be dealt with while it is still small.
Therefore the Sage never has to deal with the great; and
    so achieves greatness.
But again 'Light assent inspires little confidence
And "many easies" means many a hard.'
Therefore the Sage knows too how to make the easy diffi-
cult, and by doing so avoid all difficulties!

Commentary

The author first appropriates the maxim 'Requite
injuries with good deeds, etc.',[3] and shows how perfectly it
fits in with his own teaching. He then, as a *tour de force*,
appropriates a second and apparently contradictory proverb, with equal success.

The word *tê* ('good deeds' in the proverb) is the same as

[1] In Ch. 35 Tao itself is said to be 'flavourless'.
[2] Compare *Han Fei Tzŭ*, 38. The saying originally merely meant
'attend to troubles in time, before they get out of hand'.
[3] Confucius (*Analects* XIV. 36) criticizes this proverb and says if you
repay injuries with good deeds, how are you going to repay good
deeds?

that by which Taoists denoted the mysterious 'power' of Tao. The world laughs at Tao, the author says, and we requite this injury with the gift of *tê*. In what follows the 'easy' and 'small' is the Primal Unity underlying the apparent diversity of things. The Taoist passes as easily from the 'easy' aspect of things to their 'hard' aspect as he does from the 'hard' to the 'easy'; that is to say he is capable of seeing things as parts or as a unity, according to what the occasion requires.

CHAPTER LXIV

'What stays still is easy to hold;
Before there has been an omen it is easy to lay plans.
What is tender is easily torn,[1]
What is minute is easy to scatter.'
Deal with things in their state of not-yet-being,
Put them in order before they have got into confusion.
For 'the tree big as a man's embrace began as a tiny sprout,
The tower nine storeys high began with a heap of earth,
The journey of a thousand leagues began with what was under
 the feet'.
He who acts, harms; he who grabs, lets slip.
Therefore the Sage does not act, and so does not harm;
Does not grab, and so does not let slip.
Whereas the people of the world, at their tasks,
Constantly spoil things when within an ace of completing
 them.
'Heed the end no less than the beginning,'[2]
And your work will not be spoiled.
Therefore[3] the Sage wants only things that are unwanted,
Sets no store by products difficult to get,

 1 Reading *p'an* with the 'knife' determinative; or 'What is soft is
easily melted', if we keep the 'water' determinative.
 2 For similar sayings see *Book of History*, Legge, pp. 183 and 211.
 3 Because the 'end' (the world around us) is as important as the
'beginning' (the primal state, the One, the Whole). The Sage does
not only work through Tao; he also shows the world the degree to
which ordinary life can be moulded to the pattern of Tao.

And so teaches things untaught,
Turning all men back to the things they have left behind,[1]
That the ten thousand creatures may be restored to their Self-
 so.[2]
This he does; but dare not act.

[1] Such as walking instead of riding, used knotted ropes instead of writing, etc. See Ch. 80.
[2] To what they are of themselves, as opposed to what they are in relation to other things.

CHAPTER LXV

IN THE days of old those who practised Tao with success did not, by means of it, enlighten the people, but on the contrary sought to make them ignorant.
The more knowledge people have, the harder they are to rule.
Those who seek to rule by giving knowledge
Are like bandits preying on the land.
Those who rule without giving knowledge
Bring a stock of good fortune to the land.
To have understood the difference between these two things is to have a test and standard.
To be always able to apply this test and standard
Is called the mysterious 'power',
The mysterious 'power', so deep-penetrating,
So far-reaching,
That can follow things back——
All the way back to the Great Concordance.[1]

[1] Cf. *Chuang Tzŭ*, XII, 8.

CHAPTER LXVI

How did the great rivers and seas get their kingship over
   the hundred lesser streams?
Through the merit of being lower than they; that was how
   they got their kingship.
Therefore the Sage
In order to be above the people
Must speak as though he were lower than the people.
In order to guide them
He must put himself behind them.
Only thus can the Sage be on top and the people not be
   crushed by his weight.
Only thus can he guide, and the people not be led into
harm.
Indeed in this way everything under heaven will be glad
to be pushed by[1] him and will not find his guidance irk-
some. This he does by not striving; and because he does
not strive, none can contend with him.

[1] 'From behind'.

CHAPTER LXVII

EVERY ONE under heaven says that our Way is greatly like folly. But it is just because it is great, that it seems like folly. As for things that do not seem like folly[1]—well, there can be no question about *their* smallness!
Here are my three treasures.[2] Guard and keep them! The first is pity; the second, frugality; the third: refusal to be 'foremost of all things under heaven'.
For only he that pities is truly able to be brave;
Only he that is frugal is truly able to be profuse.
Only he that refuses to be foremost of all things
Is truly able to become chief of all Ministers.[3]
At present your bravery is not based on pity, nor your profusion on frugality, nor your vanguard on your rear;[4] and this is death. But pity cannot fight without conquering or guard without saving. Heaven arms with pity those whom it would not see destroyed.[5]

---

[1] Literally 'that seem normal'.

[2] The three rules that formed the practical, political side of the author's teaching (1) abstention from aggressive war and capital punishment, (2) absolute simplicity of living, (3) refusal to assert active authority.

[3] The phrase has exactly the same meaning as the *kuan-ch'ang* of Ch. 28.

[4] i.e. your eminence on self-effacement. This is as perilous as to leave one's line of communication undefended.

[5] Such is the sense that our author gives to the saying. It is probable, however, that it is simply a couplet from some old ritual-song (like those in the last part of the *Book of Odes*) and means 'Heaven deigned to help them; in its pity it protected them'.

Tao Tê Ching

Commentary

The opening passage cannot be rendered satisfactorily, for it depends on a series of plays on words. *Ta* (1) greatly, (2) great. *Pu-hsiao* 'below the average in capacity'; the opposite of *hsien* 'above the average in capacity'. But there is a play on *hsiao* 'average', 'normal' and *hsiao* 'small' which is sometimes written with this same character.

CHAPTER LXVIII

The best charioteers do not rush ahead;[1]
The best fighters do not make displays of wrath.[2]
The greatest conqueror wins without joining issue;
The best user of men acts as though he were their inferior.
This is called the power that comes of not contending, (competing)
Is called the capacity to use men,
The secret of being mated to heaven, to what was of old.

---

[1] Wang Pi says quite rightly that *Shih* is a 'leader' of foot-soldiers. The leaders rode in war-chariots. He also says that *wu* means 'rushing in front of the others'. Cf. *Sun Tzŭ* P'ien 9, end. The usual translation ('The best soldiers are not warlike') misses the point.
[2] *Nu* is anger shown outwardly, as by glaring, grimacing or the like.

CHAPTER LXIX

The strategists have the sayings: 'When you doubt your
ability to meet the enemy's attack, take the offensive
yourself', and 'If you doubt your ability to advance an
inch, then retreat a foot'.
This latter is what we call to march without moving,
To roll the sleeve, but present no bare arm,
The hand that seems to hold, yet has no weapon in it,
A host that can confront, yet presents no battle-front.[1]
Now the greatest of all calamities is to attack and find no
    enemy.
I can have no enemy only at the price of losing my treasure.[2]
Therefore when armies are raised and issues joined it is he
    who does not delight in war that wins.

Commentary

In the scramble for empire that marked the final phase
of the feudal period in China the watchword was 'No
enemy under heaven', i.e. each State looked forward to a
time when it should have crushed all the other States.
The Realists used this watchword in an extended application, applying it also to internal polities: the State can
tolerate no criticism or opposition. That this maxim, in
either of its senses, can only be fulfilled at the expense of
'pity' is obvious. Later editors, no longer understanding

[1] The Wang Pi commentary shows the order in which these clauses
should come.

[2] i.e. pity. Secondary sense: 'He whose enemy presents no front,
loses his booty'. For this sense of *pao* see *Kuan Tzŭ*, P'ien 17, middle.

the connotations of the phrase 'no enemy' altered the
text to 'despising one's enemy'; but Wang Pi's commentary makes it clear that he read 'no enemy' and perfectly understood what the phrase denoted.

The two strategists quoted at the beginning of the
chapter would appear to be Wang Liao and I Liang, cf.
Lü Shih Ch'un Ch'iu, 99. A book by the latter still survived
at the beginning of the Christian era, see *Han Shu* XXX,
fol. 26.

CHAPTER LXX

My words are very easy to understand and very easy to put into practice. Yet no one under heaven understands them; no one puts them into practice. But my words have an ancestry, my deeds have a lord;[1] and it is precisely because men do not understand this that they are unable to understand me.

Few then understand me; but it is upon this very fact that my value depends. It is indeed in this sense[2] that 'the Sage wears hair-cloth on top, but carries jade underneath his dress'.

[1] To have 'neither ancestors nor lord' was to be a wild man, a savage. This is a metaphorical way of saying that all the Sage did and said was related to a definite system of thought.

[2] In this sense, and not in the sense that he flies in panic from the horrors of the world. Rich people, in times of tumult, dressed up as peasants and hid their jade treasures under their clothes. Metaphorically 'to wear haircloth' etc., came to mean 'to hide one's light under a bushel', 'to keep one's knowledge to oneself'.

CHAPTER LXXI

'To know when one does not know is best.
To think one knows when one does not know is a dire
disease.
Only he who recognizes this disease as a disease
Can cure himself of the disease.'
The Sage's way of curing disease
Also consists in making people recognize their diseases as
diseases and thus ceasing to be diseased.

Commentary

The best way to explain this chapter is to paraphrase it.
The people of the world, the author says, have a saying
to the effect that it is best of all never to think that one
knows when one doesn't know, for to think one knows
when in reality one is ignorant is a dire disease; most
people, however, are bound to suffer to some extent from
this disease, and if they will only recognize the fact that
they suffer from it, they will take steps to extend their
knowledge and so protect themselves from the 'disease'.

'Well, the whole of my teaching', he replies, 'consists simply in making people recognize that what they
mistake for conditions of health are really conditions of
disease; that their virtues (humanity, morality, observance
of etiquette, etc.) are really vices, that what they prize
(luxury, fame, power, etc.) is really worthless.

In the last chapter the author says that his style seems
obscure, yet to anyone possessing the clue is perfectly
lucid. In this chapter he supplies the classic example of
this 'enigmatic lucidity'.

CHAPTER LXXII

NEVER MIND if the people are not intimidated by your authority. A Mightier Authority[1] will deal with them in the end. Do not narrow their dwellings[2] or harass their lives;[3] and for the very reason that you do not harrass them, they will cease to turn from[4] you. Therefore the Sage knows himself[5] but does not show himself. Knows his own value, but does not put himself on high. Truly, 'he rejects that but takes this'.[6]

[1] Heaven. Cf. *I Chou Shu*, P'ien 67.
[2] i.e. put them in prison. See textual notes.
[3] Literally, 'that whereby they live', their livelihoods. The author is thinking of heavy taxation and the like.
[4] There is a pun on 'harass' and 'turn from'; see textual notes. The root means originally 'to press down from above'. Hence (1) to oppress (2) to have food crammed into one, to be 'fed up', to turn away in disgust.
[5] i.e. knows his own power, but does not display it.
[6] See Ch. 12.

CHAPTER LXXIII

He whose braveness lies in daring, slays.
He whose braveness lies in not daring,[1] gives life.
Of these two, either may be profitable or unprofitable.
But 'Heaven hates what it hates;
None can know the reason why'.[2]
Wherefore the Sage, too, disallows it.
For it is the way of Heaven not to strive but none the less
    to conquer,
Not to speak, but none the less to get an answer,
Not to beckon; yet things come to it of themselves.
Heaven is like one who says little,[3] yet none the less has
    laid his plans.
Heaven's net is wide;
Coarse are the meshes, yet nothing slips through.

---

[1] i.e. in not daring to slay.
[2] Heaven hates the shedding of blood (i.e. it is 'against nature'), and those who ignore the will of Heaven are bound to be trapped at last in the meshes of Fate. This is the traditional pacifist argument of the Mo Tzŭ school, which our author is here able to utilize by identifying Heaven with Tao. For 'Heaven hates what it hates. . . .' Cf. *Lieh Tzŭ*, VI. 5.
[3] See textual notes.

CHAPTER LXXIV

THE PEOPLE are not frightened of death. What then is the
use of trying to intimidate them with the death-penalty?
And even supposing people were generally frightened of
death and did not regard it as an everyday thing, which of
us would dare to seize them and slay them?[1] There is the
Lord of Slaughter[2] always ready for this task, and to do it
in his stead is like thrusting oneself into the master-
carpenter's place and doing his chipping for him. Now
'he who tries to do the master-carpenter's chipping for him
is lucky if he does not cut his hand'.[3]

[1] i.e. even supposing the death-penalty really had the effect of
scaring people and keeping down crime, is it fair to ask anyone to
undertake such a task?
[2] i.e. Heaven, or its agents (pestilence, famine, lightning, earth-
quake, etc.).
[3] Adaptation of a proverb meaning 'let every man stick to his task'.

CHAPTER LXXV

THE PEOPLE starve because those above them eat too much tax-grain. That is the only reason why they starve. The people are difficult to keep in order because those above them interfere. That is the only reason why they are so difficult to keep in order. The people attach no importance to death, because those above them are too grossly absorbed in the pursuit of life. That is why they[1] attach no importance to death. And indeed, in that their hearts are so little set on life they are superior to those who set store by life.[2]

---

[1] The people.
[2] i.e. are superior to their rulers; so that there is no chance of the state being well governed.

CHAPTER LXXVI

WHEN HE is born, man is soft and weak; in death he becomes stiff and hard. The ten thousand creatures and all plants and trees while they are alive are supple and soft, but when they are dead they become brittle and dry. Truly, what is stiff and hard is a 'companion of death'; what is soft and weak is a 'companion of life'.[1] Therefore 'the weapon that is too hard[2] will be broken, the tree that has the hardest wood will be cut down'. Truly, the hard and mighty are cast down; the soft and weak set on high.

[1] Cf. Ch. 50.
[2] The proverb exists in several forms, and the text has been tampered with, so that the exact reading is uncertain. But the general sense is quite clear. Cf. *Lieh Tzŭ* II. 16.

CHAPTER LXXVII

HEAVEN'S WAY is like the bending of a bow.[1] When a bow is bent the top comes down and the bottom-end comes up. So too does Heaven take away from those who have too much, and give to those that have not enough. But if it is Heaven's way to take from those who have too much and give to those who have not enough, this is far from being man's way. He takes away from those that have not enough in order to make offering to those who already have too much. One there is and one only, so rich that he can afford to make offerings to all under heaven. Who is this? It is the possessor of Tao. If, then, the Sage 'though he controls does not lean, and when he has achieved his aim does not linger',[2] it is because he does not wish to reveal himself as better than others.

[1] Not in the act of stringing it, but in the act of shooting an arrow from it. There is no reason at all to suppose with Wilhelm that the composite, double-bending bow is meant.
[2] Over the scene of his triumph. Cf. Ch. 2. If he leaned, the people would know who it was that was controlling them; if he lingered, they would recognize who it was that had done the work. They would regard him as 'better', 'superior'; and to allow oneself to be so regarded is to sin against 'Heaven's way' and so lose one's power.

CHAPTER LXXVIII

NOTHING UNDER heaven is softer or more yielding than water;[1] but when it attacks things hard and resistant there is not one of them that can prevail. For they can find no way of altering[2] it. That the yielding conquers the resistant and the soft conquers the hard is a fact known by all men, yet utilized by none. Yet it is in reference to this that the Sage[3] said 'Only he who has accepted the dirt of the country can be lord of its soil-shrines;[4] only he who takes upon himself the evils of the country can become a king among those what dwell under heaven.' Straight words seem crooked.[5]

---

[1] Cf. Ch. 12; also 43.

[2] i.e. damaging.

[3] Lao Tan. Cf. *Chuang Tzŭ*, XXXIII. 5.

[4] Reference to a custom similar to the 'seizin' of medieval Europe, whereby a new tenant took a clod of earth in his hand to symbolize possession of the soil. The Chinese expression *han hou*, generally used in this connexion, suggests that the clod was originally held by the new feudal lord or tenant between his teeth—a sort of symbolic eating. Thus he absorbed the 'virtue' of the soil.

[5] Seem, as we should say, to be paradoxes.

CHAPTER LXXIX

To ALLAY the main discontent, but only in a manner that will certainly produce further discontents can hardly be called successful. Therefore the Sage behaves like the holder of the left-hand tally, who stays where he is and does not go round making claims on people. For he who has the 'power' of Tao is the Grand Almoner; he who has not the 'power' is the Grand Perquisitor. 'It is Heaven's way, without distinction of persons, to keep the good perpetually supplied.'

Commentary

The meaning of this chapter, which exemplifies the author's literary procedure at its subtlest, can best be made clear by a paraphrase.

It is no use trying to govern in the ordinary way, by laws and restrictions, penalties and rewards. For at any given moment (see Ch. XXIX) some of your subjects will be 'blowing hot while others are blowing cold. Some will be loading while others are tilting'. You will only be able to content some by discontenting others. In fact it is no use trying to *ho* (fit together, harmonize). Thus the Sage is like the holder of the left-hand half of a tally, who is ready to give out what is due (i.e. is ready to vouchsafe the bounties of Tao), but does not go round trying to fit (*ho*) his half of the tally to someone else's half, as the creditor does. He is indeed like the officer who gives public assistance (pun on *ch'i* 'tally' and *ch'ieh* 'help', 'assist')[1] to

[1] See textual notes.

the needy and aged; whereas the ordinary ruler is a sort of Grand Tithe-Collector. In the author's application of the proverb which he quotes at the end of the chapter, 'the good' of course means the Taoist Sage, whom Heaven supplies with the inexhaustible treasures of Tao, so that, though a debtor, the Sage is in a position to be always 'giving out', to be always 'meeting claims'. For the origin of the terms employed, see additional notes.

CHAPTER LXXX

GIVEN A small country with few inhabitants,[1] he could bring it about that though there should be among the people contrivances requiring ten times, a hundred times less labour,[2] they would not use them. He could bring it about that the people would be ready to lay down their lives and lay them down again[3] in defence of their homes, rather than emigrate.[4] There might still be boats and carriages, but no one would go in them; there might still be weapons of war but no one would drill with them. He could bring it about that 'the people should have no use for any form of writing save knotted ropes,[5] should be contented with their food, pleased with their clothing, satisfied with their homes, should take pleasure in their rustic tasks. The next place might be so near at hand that one could hear the cocks crowing in it, the dogs

[1] i.e. no need for a large country and many inhabitants, which was what the princes of the world pined for.

[2] Cf. *Shang Tzŭ*, I. I, and *Chan Kuo Ts'ê* VI. 26, where the principle is laid down that new mechanical contrivances may be accepted if they are ten times more efficient than the old. For the Taoist objection to mechanical contrivances see *Chuang Tzŭ* XII. II, already quoted.

[3] For *ch'ung-ssŭ* in the sense of 'die twice over' compare *Lü Shih Ch'un Ch'iu*, 131, end: 'Every one has to die once, but it may be truly said that Ch'ing Fêng died twice over'.

[4] Cf. Introduction, p. 80.

[5] One knots ropes as an aid to one's *own* memory (compare our 'tying a knot in one's handkerchief'); whereas one writes contracts down in order to make other people fulfil them. That, I think, is why 'knotting' belongs to the Golden Age. I doubt whether the *quipus* of South American Indians are relevant.

barking; but the people would grow old and die without ever having been there'.[1]

---

[1] The passage in inverted commas occurs (with trifling differences) in *Chuang Tzŭ* (X. 3) as a description of life under the rule of the legendary agricultural Sage Shên-nung. The whole chapter can be understood in the past, present or future tense, as the reader desires.

CHAPTER LXXXI

True words are not fine-sounding;
Fine-sounding words are not true.
The good man does not prove by argument;
And he who proves by argument[1] is not good.
True wisdom is different from much learning;
Much learning means little wisdom.
The Sage has no need to hoard;
When his own last scrap has been used up on behalf of others,
Lo, he has more than before!
When his own last scrap has been used up in giving to others,
Lo, his stock is even greater than before![2]
For Heaven's way is to sharpen without cutting,[3]
And the Sage's way is to act without striving.

---

[1] i.e. the 'sophist'; see Introduction, p. 64.
[2] Adaptation of a saying that occurs in several forms. Cf. *Chuang Tzŭ*, XXI, end.
[3] To achieve the end without using the material means.

ADDITIONAL NOTE ON INTRODUCTION

P. 26 The 'shih' (medium)

The question of the *shih* is one of considerable interest to the anthropologist. It appears that such an institution, though familiar enough in funerary ritual and indeed still surviving even in remote parts of Europe, has seldom save in China been extended to sacrificial ritual. My authority for saying this is E. O. James's very careful and scholarly work, *Origins of Sacrifice*, where there is no mention of such an institution. I do not mean of course that it is rare for anyone taking part in sacrifice to be 'possessed' by a spirit. The *shaman* is a common enough feature at sacrificial ceremonies. But the typical characteristic of the *shaman* is that he dances; whereas the typical characteristic of the *shih* is that he remains immobile.[1] It follows from this that field-workers in anthropology could not fail to notice a *shaman*; but might easily fail to notice or at any rate understand the significance of a *shih*. It would surprise me if it did not turn out that the *shih* is a much less unique institution than one might at first sight suppose. Some account of this custom may be found in Maspero's *La Chine Antique*. See also Kano Naoyoshi's *Shinagaku Bunso*, pp. 94-128 (in Japanese).

---

[1] Not, of course, during the whole ceremony, but during the major part of it.

ADDITIONAL NOTES ON TRANSLATION

Chapter I

The original meaning of *ku* is 'old'. Hence 'well-established'; hence 'true'. It is put in front of a proverb or accepted maxim after a demonstration that what is propounded does not conflict with this proverb. It often has a sense transitional between 'Truly' and 'therefore'. But it would be possible to quote many passages in early Chinese literature where 'therefore', in such contents, is an impossible rendering; and this is often the case in the *Tao Tê Ching*. In later times *ku* with determinative 31 was reserved for the sense 'truly' and *ku* with determinative 66 always meant 'therefore'. For the characters, see textual notes.

'Ultimate results': *chiao*. The character is exceedingly common in early texts in the sense 'to seek' (almost always 'to seek a blessing from Heaven'). It does not occur in the quite different sense which it has here till *Lieh Tzŭ*, which is, at the earliest, a work of the late 3rd century B.C. This fact is important in connection with the dating of the *Tao Tê Ching*. See my article in the *Bulletin of the School of Oriental Studies*, 1934.

Chapter XIII

For *ching* in the sense 'beside oneself' cf. the story (*Kuo Yü*, 18) of Ho-lü, famous for his moral zest. On hearing of one good deed this monarch would become so excited that he was *jo ching* 'as it were beside himself'.

Tao Tê Ching

In Chinese the word *shên* 'body' also means 'self', and as this word was used to translate the Sanskrit *ātman* ('self'). Many Buddhist texts which deal with *Atman* ('personality') and not with the physical body look in their Chinese dress uncommonly like this passage of the *Tao Tê Ching*. Thus the Chinese version of the Sutra of Dharmapada Parables[1] says: 'Of all evils under heaven none is worse than having a *shên.*' It was natural that the Chinese (and Western writers in their wake) should take *shên* not in its real sense of *Ātman*, 'self', but as meaning body. Thus Tao-shih[2] in 659 A.D., commenting on this Dharmapada passage, explains it by quoting *Tao Tê Ching*, Ch. XIII, a reference which is in reality quite irrelevant.

Chapter XX

Line 12. Literally 'going up to the Spring Terrace'. This is generally taken merely to mean going up on to a terrace to admire the view. But 'Spring Terrace' balances 'Great Sacrificial-banquet', and must also be the name of a religious ceremony. Now we know from the *Ch'ing Chia Lu*[3] of Ku Lu that 'in the second or third month the richer and more public-spirited among the local gentry pile up a terrace on some open piece of unused ground and provide money for a play. Men and women look on together. It is called the Spring Terrace Play, and is intended to ensure fertility of the crops'. The terrace was of course not intended as a stage, but was a raised bank for the audience to sit on. The fact that men and women, contrary to Chinese custom, sat together indicates that the Spring

1 Takakusu, IV, 595a   2 *Ibidem*, LIV, p. 63.
3 I know this book only in quotation.

Terrace was originally the scene of a kind of carnival, a period of authorized license intended, as such festivals always are, to promote the fertility of the fields. It is of course a far cry from the 18th century (Ku Lu's period) to the 3rd century B.C.; but I think it may in any case be taken as certain that some kind of carnival is referred to.

Chapter XXI

A 'charge' (*ming*) consists of the 'life-giving words' that a general addresses to troops before a battle or the instructions that a king gives to a new feudal lord or minister. The object of this charge is to 'animate' the troops, lord, or minister, with a particular purpose. For this reason he speaks 'words of good cheer', which is the root meaning of the character I have translated 'cheers onward'. The 'ten thousand things are compared to troops in whose ears the general's (i.e. Tao's) orders of the day' still ring.

Of the three characters given for *fu* in the textual notes, the first simply means 'a big (i.e. adult) man'. The second, 'the hand with the stick', i.e. the person who beats one at one's tribal initiation, and so (at a later stage of society when fatherhood began to take its place beside motherhood as a known and recognized relationship) 'the father'. The third character ('use' plus 'hand with stick') means 'the name given to an adult for ordinary use', and it is only as a phonetic equivalent that it stands for 'grown man'. The most accurate way to write 'men' in the sense of 'soldiers' would be to use the first of the three characters.

1 There is no evidence of violent initiation in China and I now (1948) feel doubtful about this explanation of the character.

Chapter XXVII

Hsi, 'to resort to'.

This character has two distinct sets of usages, which do not seem to be etymologically akin. (1) fold, double, repeat, imitate. With this series we are not here concerned. (2) It serves as an intensive to *ju* 'to go into', with the meanings 'go into and stay there', 'establish oneself in', 'put oneself under the protection of'; with a hostile sense, 'invade'. For parallels, see *Chuang Tzŭ*, XV, 2, 'Evil humours cannot *establish* themselves (in such a man)'; balances *ju*, to enter. *Ibidem*, VI. 4. 'It was by getting Tao that 'K'an-p'i *established* himself on Mt. K'un-lun.' *Ibidem*, XX. 7. 'The swallow though afraid of men *establishes* itself among them. . . .' *Huai-nan Tzŭ* VI. 'The bears slink into their mountain caverns, the tiger and leopard *establish* themselves (i.e. ensconce themselves) in their lairs, and dare not so much as utter a sound.' *Kuo Yü*, 8, 'When a large country is well ruled and a small country resorts to the large one for protection. . . .'

From the basic sense 'going in and stopping in' is derived, I think, that of 'adopting' a new form of attire. Cf. *Chan Kuo Ts'ê*, VI. 19.

Chapter XXXI

'In peace the left-hand side is the place of honour. . . .' We know too that circumambulatory rites were in civil life performed clockwise; but in war, anti-clockwise. The distinction is a very important one in all primitive ritual, cf. *I Chou Shu* 32. 'It is the way of Heaven to prefer the right; the sun and moon travel westward. It is the way of earth to prefer the left; the watercourses flow to the east[1] . . . In rites of good omen, circumambulation is to the left; it follows the way of earth, in order that the performers themselves may be benefited. In ceremonies of war, circumambulation is to the right; it follows the way of Heaven, in order that the weapons may gain in sharpness.'

Chapter XXXVIII

The *tao* (doctrine) of which foreknowledge was the flower is of course not Taoism, but may well be the branch of Confucianism represented, for example, by the *Doctrine of the Mean* (paragraph 24): 'The way of complete fulfilment (of one's own nature) leads to knowledge of what is to come.' Support for the idea of the Sage as prophet was found in *Analects* II. 23.[2] See also *Lü Shih Ch'un Ch'iu*, P'ien 85, where a whole section is devoted to foreknowledge. The Dualists and systematizers of theories based on the Five Elements also went in for prophecy. It is unlikely that diviners by the *Book of Changes* are meant, for this work is seldom alluded to by writers of the third century, and did not become part of the Confucian curriculum till the Han dynasty. As the clauses which go before are directed against Confucianism, it seems likely that it is a Confucian doctrine that is here condemned.

Chapter XXXIX

'Direct their people.'
Chêng ('cowry-shell' underneath 'to divine') passes in a particularly interesting manner from an auguristic to a

1 Read *tung*, not *chung*.
2 'Can ten generations hence be foreknown?'

moral meaning. In the Honan Oracle-records (12th-11th century B.C.), where it occurs thousands of times, it means to ask for an oracular response. When the *Book of Changes* began to be used as a text in conjunction with divination by the yarrow-stalks, the term *chêng* took on a number of technical significations, still purely auguristic. When however (perhaps in the 4th century B.C.) the *Book of Changes* was reinterpreted in a metaphysical and ethical sense, *chêng* was by a play upon words[1] taken in the sense 'straight', as opposed to crooked, and so (in a moral sense) 'upright', In the 3rd century B.C. the old auguristic meaning was practically obsolete, and the character simply means 'straight' or 'to straighten' morally or meta-phorically as opposed to straightening physically.

'Enumerate the parts of a carriage. . . .'

Buddhist writers[2] frequently use a parable which at first sight looks as though it were closely connected with this passage, and the late Sir Charles Eliot[3] went so far as to believe that the *Tao Tê Ching* was here influenced by Buddhism. There is however no real connection. The Buddhist argument runs: just as when the various parts of a carriage have been removed one by one, there is no carriage left, so when the various component parts of the human aggregate have been removed one by one, there is no *sat* ('being') left. Whereas here the argument (like

[1] i.e. by identifying it with *chêng*, 'straight', originally written with quite a different character. For the two characters, see textual notes.

[2] *Samyutta Nikāya*, V. 10. 6. *Samyuktāgama*, Takakusu, II. 327 b. *Milinda Questions*, Sacred Books of the East XXXV, 43-45, *Mahāparinir-vāna Sūtra*, Ch. 27, *Prajñāpāramitā Sāstra*, Ch. 31.

[3] *Hinduism and Buddhism*, III. 246.

that of *Chuang Tzŭ* XXV. 10) is that the whole cannot be known by separately knowing the parts.

Chapter XLI

'. . . Looks flimsy.' The original meaning of *t'ou* is to pull, to force (of doors, etc.). Hence (1) 'a forcer of doors', a thief. (2) (as here) 'able to be forced', flimsy.[1]

For *yü* (here translated 'faded') applied to colours, see *Huai-nan Tzŭ*, 20, par. 6. For *chih* applied to substances of natural as opposed to artificial colour, see *Ta Tai Li Chi*, P'ien 72, fol. 4 verso.

Chapter XLII

The saying 'The man of violence never yet came to a good end . . .' occurs in the so-called Inscription on the Statue, known to us in various forms. I here combine the versions in *K'ung Tzŭ Chia Yü*, XI, and *Shuo Yüan* X, neither of which is satisfactory in itself. The mouth of the statue (which is supposed to have stood in the Great Ancestral Hall of the Chous) was sealed with a triple seal. On its back was an inscription in homely, countryside language, the burden of which was 'least said soonest mended'. But at the end comes a series of maxims for the Quietist ruler: 'The man of violence never yet came to a good end. He that delights in victory meets his match at last. As surely as bandits hate their chief, so do the people of a country resent whatever is over them. The man of discernment, knowing that a kingdom cannot be mounted, gets under it; knowing that the people cannot be led he keeps behind them. . . . Play obstinately the female's part,

[1] In this sense sometimes written with the 'woman' determinative.

cling to the under place; and no one will be able to contend with you. All men turn to *that*; I only keep *this*. All men vainly stray; I alone am unmoved. I keep my knowledge to myself; I discuss the mysteries of my craft with none. . . . If the Yang-tzŭ and the Yellow River have mastery over the hundred streams, it is because they humble themselves and take the low ground. It is heaven's way to show no partiality,[1] but ever to side with the good[2] man.'

There is some reason to suppose that the Inscription on the Statue is one of the 'Six Inscriptions of the Yellow Ancestor', a work still current in the Han dynasty. See Ku Chieh-kang, *Ku Shih Pien*, Vol. IV, p. 501.

Chapter XLVI

Chiao means here not the 'outskirts' of the kingdom, but the mound on the outskirts of the capital, scene of the Great Sacrifice (cf. Maspero, *La Chine Antique*, p. 225 seq.) which inaugurated the season's agriculture. To let weeds grow on this mound was a sacrilege;[3] and to breed war-horses upon it, a double profanation. For the Great Sacrifice is essentially connected with peace.

'Lure.' The root means 'fluttering' like a bird. Hence (1) to set a trap, to lure. (2) to be caught in meshes (of the law), a criminal. (3) that which involves one in such meshes, a crime.

Chapter LIII

Chieh-jan, 'the least scrap of'. Cf. *Lieh Tzŭ*, IV. 2.

[1] No personal favour.   [2] i.e. with the Quietist.

[3] Compare *Hsün Tzŭ*, P'ien 16, end: 'He who does not sweep the droppings at home is not likely to notice that weeds run riot on the *chiao* mound.'

Tao Tê Ching

'The least scrap of any existing thing, the least whisper of sound. . . .' It can also be used of time: 'A hill-way used only for the least little while turns into a well-defined path. . . . (*Mencius* VII. Part II, 21.)

Chapter LVIII

The phrase translated 'shapes the corners without lopping' has a long history, and has been put to a variety of different uses. It primarily describes jade, which is 'cornered without being jagged' (see *K'ung Tzŭ Chia Yü*, P'ien 36) and thus becomes the symbol of morality, which is scrupulous without being prickly', or of conduct (*hsing*), as in *Kuan Tzŭ*, 39. For other applications see *Hsün Tzŭ*, 3, and 30 which is a variant on the *Chia Yü* passage.

Chapter LXXIX

It was believed[1] that in the time of the ancient Sages a certain proportion of land in each village had been set aside as 'common land' and its produce handed over to officials to be used for communal purposes, such as (1) the support of the aged and needy, (2) the support of officials. Under the Yin dynasty, it was said, this system was known as 'labour-loaning', because the villagers lent their labour to the community. This term came to have the meaning 'assistance', because the needy were 'helped' out of the fund so established. But it also came to mean 'taxation', because the produce was handed over to and in part used by officials. The author here uses the term assistance ('Almoner', literally 'Assister') in the first sense. In the

[1] What relation these beliefs bear to any actual, ancient system of tithe it is hard to say.

255

Chou dynasty, it was said, various local systems of tithe were replaced by a 'general' system, and the word 'general' (*ch'ê*) came to mean tithing, tax-exaction. This is the word here used in the phrase *ssŭ-ch'ê*, 'controller of taxes, perquisitor'. The saying quoted in the end of the chapter (It is Heaven's way . . .) is from the Inscription on the Statue (see Ch. XLII, additional notes); but it occurs elsewhere, in a variety of forms.

Tallies played in the life of the early Chinese the same part that tickets, cheques, etc., do in Europe to-day. They were used as 'passes' of admission to fortified places, as 'tickets' entitling the owners to a share in sacrificial meat, as 'cheques' in commerce. The importance of the tally in actual life is attested by the great variety of metaphorical senses in which the expression 'fitting the tallies' is used by early writers. Thus Mencius (IV. 2. 1) says that the methods of all the Sages, both former and latter, 'fit like tallies'. The Codifiers said that if everything helpful and everything inimical to the State were defined, the ruler would merely have to 'fit the tallies' by allotting rewards and punishments according to the Code. It is used of deeds that are 'as good as' words, of theories that work in practice, and finally at a later date, of the successful 'fitting together' of ingredients in alchemy.

TEXTUAL NOTES

Ch. 1 故; 固. 徼. Ch. 2 較. 形 was merely substituted to secure an extra rhyme. Ch. 10 營 for 魂, as frequently in old texts, with the meaning 惑 'astray'. Ch. 13 omit 寵 before 為; it is a gloss on 之. Ch. 21 'warriors'. 夫, 甫 and 父 are all etymologically the same, coming from a root meaning 'adult man'. Its 'charge'. . . . 名 in the sense of 命. 令 is cognate; the original root was *mling*. Ch. 25. Play on 大 and 達, which were both pronounced approximately *d'ât*. 域 in sense of 或, logical 'divisions' (?). Ch. 32 read 道 常 而 無 名. Ch. 34 read 而 不 有. 衣 被 . . . Ch. 39 貞 and 正. Ch. 42 read 者 得, omitting 不, which has crept in owing to the negative in the original proverb. Ch. 59 read 服, in the same sense as in 服 藥, etc. Ch. 72 壓 and 厭. 狎 in the sense of 狹. The two words are however etymologically the same; see Karlgren, *Anal. Dict*, p. 123, Ch. 73 繟 in sense of 嘽.

Ch. 79: Pun on 絜 and 挈. The original of course facilitated the play on words by merely writing 刧.

INDEX

Index

Index

Index